SEND IT BY PIGEON

How our family found and purchased property on a semi seculded island.

Bruce William Thibodeau

Bruce William Thibodeau, Sanford MI.

For permission requests, email
Bruce Thibodeau
fruitlandservices@gmail.com

Company names and Individual names used with
the kind permission of owners and individuals.

Front Cover Design by Bruce Thibodeau.
Book Design by Bruce Thibodeau

First Print Edition 2020

ISBN-13: 978-0-578-65945-9

Cover design by: Bruce Thibodeau
Library of Congress Control Number: 2020904453
Printed in the United States of America

I would like to dedicate this book.
Perhaps I shouldn't?
Nah, I will, to all the readers.
I hope you enjoy it, find it entertaining, and if lucky, a little educational.

A special thank you to the few friends I have,
My multiple enemies who wish ill of me,
And my family for not to this point of writing, killing me.
I know I often poke fun at others, and it is a good thing they have thick skin.

A special thank you to my deceased Mother-in-Law
Julia Jenkins
I wish she was here to see it.

Acknowledgments

I would like to thank the following people for helping to make this book become a reality, without whose help we could not have made our dream become a reality. Along with those who contributed in various ways through assisting myself and my family in this grand adventure to this point.

First, my family for tolerating my insanity and schemes not to mention providing me all the support.

Second would be my friends, who helped remind me to complete something instead of starting it and forgetting about it.

Third, I would like to thank the friends we have made and those who helped in various ways.

Sheila & Henry Hyde
Without the help, we may still be wandering around lost in the woods looking at survey stakes.

Clover & Joe Schlund
For the kindness and help with offering so much including directions, water, and suggestions of who to talk to concerning various things pertaining to the island.

Larry & Missy Phillips

For the help in learning about the areas of the island, directions to places on the island, information on multiple aspects of the island, not to mention the wonderful hospitality and coffee.

Jeffrey Liedel

For the help in providing information about the area of our property and answering silly questions concerning the island.

Barry and Elizabeth Sova

For the support and continued commitment to helping me get this thing put together. Not to mention the multiple years of friendship.

Special thanks to

Hawks Landing, Bois Blanc Island Real Estate, Island Contractors, and Plaunt Transportation

Without these businesses this story would not be possible for multiple reasons.

CONTENTS

INTRODUCTION

From a cold winters morning, waiting on a teenager on through to the plans to eventually sell our home and build a new one, follow along with me as I explain the crazy way I found and purchased property on an island.

Pull up a stump and relax as I take you on an adventure with our family. From the intial discovery of finding a property for sale on a semi seculded island that we had never heard of or even knew existed. I mean honestly what could go wrong?

On through the processes we underwent to do the research on the island and the property itself. The sources we used, the people we spoke too. All in order to try to ensure that the decision we were making would result in our happieness with the decision.

I hope you find the story as enjoyable, entertaining and at times funny as we ourselves have. Looking back on the past year since we found this property and purchased it. We have if nothing else began and adventure of our lifetime, and set underway a story that will transend generations of our family in the future.

INTRODUCTION

PREFACE

Buying property sight unseen is not for the feint of heart. This book is written to try to give those of you out there who may ever consider doing as we did, an understanding that it can be done.

However it aslo highlights the work that goes into it and the fact that you will never be one hundred percent positive your purchase will be successful however it will help you to feel better about your decision should you follow through with it as we did.

Should any of you do as we did and purchase property sight unseen, I wish you all the luck and hope your as fortunate as we have been.

CHAPTER ONE

Down the Rabbit's Hole

This all began on a long winter day in the year 2019. Okay to be fair it was not day it was early morning. However, it still does not matter where it began or perhaps it does. Anyhow getting back on task this is the story of how one man aged almost 50 lost his mind. His wife idley sat beside nodding and understanding. How he also recruited all but one of his adult children. Into a grand adventure to make a story for many lifetimes. So back to the story.

I turned 50 this past year. I have no midlife crisis of wishing I had done X, or Y, and I am pretty sure I probably did Z already anyhow. What I have had is a pattern emerge in my life. I am drawn to the idea of islands and seclusion. At eight years old on our families way to North Bay, Ontario, we stopped for lunch in a pull off along a lake. Out in this lake was a granite rock island. On that rock stood a two story house. I sat and watched that house pondering many things. How did they get back and forth? How did they get food and other stuff? This house no longer had windows or doors. It had been vacant for a long time. Yet, it was appealing to me. Over the years, I have always thought of that house.

Another island house that had held my interest was one I discovered when a friend and I dropped kayaks into a small lake, not too far from where we lived. We had seen the island, and I wanted to paddle around it. As we got closer to it I saw there was a cabin, all alone on the island, a dock, a large front porch, and a very large for sale sign. I watched that house for four years before it eventually sold. I have always been interested in small islands. Now let me return to the way I lost my mind and the story of how it happened and turned out. Well turned out up to now. After all, I am living this story as it is still ongoing.

So one early winter morning in 2019, our youngest daughter of the age of just turned sixteen was up and about one morning to get herself prepared for her high school bowling competition and I was sipping coffee while waiting for her so I could go off to mentor other high school students in Robotics. However, she was taking longer than usual. I began trying to entertain myself. Which can be a very dangerous thing for a man at a computer to do, especially if he has only had one or two cups of coffee into his morning.

I began to ponder, "I wonder what properties the Department of Natural Resources has up for auction this year?" I found myself at the DNR website looking at properties. There was nothing in Midland County Michigan where we live, at least none that interested me. Next, I checked Gladwin, Clare, and Isabella Counties. Still nothing of interest. Our daughter was still off doing whatever teenage girls do to get themselves ready. As this is our third daughter, I knew I had time yet. I then decided to go and look at what the state had for sale on open purchase.

Midland county began the locations, then expanding one county at a time from east to west. Soon the lower peninsula was gone. I had found nothing in any form of price range or area I found appealing let alone interesting. I took the leap and crossed the Mighty Mac. (For all of you non native Michigan people, the Mackinac Bridge.) As I scrolled down the list of properties I glimpsed a property, four lots, a little less than a half acre for $1,500. I paused, a lot that size would be good for camping. Heck you could park a camper on it or a couple even. The price would be worth it.

So I looked at it some more. Then I pulled up some satellite imagery. Then I pulled up some tax information that I found access too. Then I found it was in a subdivision. Yet the imagery showed it predominantly woods. So I pulled up the subdivision information off the State of Michigan's web site. I found the subdivision had been created nearly 100 years ago in 1920. I then contacted our son. Asked him what he thought. As we both discussed it, we both agreed it looked like it had an awful low spot that would likely hold water a good portion of the year, which could be really bad. It would also have a potential for drawing biting, and other flying insects. Known as Michigan's Vampire Birds, or as some call them mosquitoes and their smaller cousins the "Son of a Bitch, where the hell did all these things come from.", known to some as black flies.

During this I scrolled a bit more and found nearly one and a half acres for a mere $2,500. Now I knew the one I had just seen although on a road in place already had an issue. So I began to ponder why is this other one nearly three times as much land only $1,000 more?

I looked and I looked. The land appeared higher than the first property. It had trees on it, it was not too far from a home or cabin already in existence. So I began digging

3

more. I told our son to look at that one. He agreed it looked better to him, and there was a higher topographical line running through the edge of the property showing it was higher than the other areas around it. However we had no idea if it was perhaps all swamp. Not to mention at the price although very reasonable, would take just about all our tax return to purchase half of it.

If our son was interested and he agreed to put money in for the other half we could perhaps afford it. So I looked a bit more and discovered that this piece consisted of four-teen lots. Now I am not too sharp in the mathematics de-partment yet I was able to devise that this would be seven lots each if divided by two. Or if I had the other kids inter-ested it would be cheaper yet.

Since my wife and I have discussed time and again of sell-ing our home when the youngest one leaves, going and buying a piece of property for parking a fifth wheel on, or building a smaller home, where we could enjoy the grand-kids and a simpler life. I thought perhaps it was time I take that thought a bit more seriously. I decided to contact our other daughter whom I thought might also be interested in this idea. It only took a few minutes to have her interested. This made it a three way split. So doing a bit of math again, I determined the cost divided by three and four lots each.

I then inquired into our third daughter's interest, with the option of two lots for her and her husband, which is about the same size as the property that the home they own is on currently. She showed no real interest. Leading me to decide a three way split with a communal set of two lots for visitors.

At this time, I should also state, I do have disabilities which does limit my physical ability to do hard physical labor for periods of time. I am good for short periods of time. However, the result is an hour or two of something most consider a workout and I spend the next day or two pretty much incapable of doing more than getting up moving around a room, and sitting down. From which getting up again can be a challenge and adventure in relearning what it is pain is like.

So cutting grass and using a weed trimmer is about my limit, which has taken me a few years to learn. Running a chainsaw for about thirty minutes to an hour, and my daily limit is reached. So, again as we are looking at this property from satellite I am thinking. "This is pretty thick. We would need to cut a road into the property and then clean it up." I reminded our son and daughter of the work it would take. I am after all wanting to be upfront and honest.

Everyone is showing interest, and so it begins. "Well, Dad, I am at work, but if you want to keep yourself occupied and do the research, I am seriously interested," were the words of our son. "Well, Dad if you and Mom are interested and Rion is too, then I would be interested too," was our 22 year old daughters response. This was all fine and such. However, the boss was still in bed. I remind you that this process began with a teenager dragging her feet and a bored 50 year old man. All of this has transpired within about an hour and a half.

So I await my wife, the boss, the individual who is slightly like a brown bear when woken from hibernation. You never know if you will get your face ripped off or just looked at with a glare out of the corner of her eye, knowing she is pondering killing you for food or spending the energy that would take to better look elsewhere for a more filling and less energy using meal. I have survived in this marriage, however, for twenty years at this point and learned that if I sit quietly, until the bear has satisfied its hunger, that it is then content to listen while sitting quietly allowing its body to acclimate to the fact that she has woken up and that there are things to do. She is usually a bit more approachable then. However, being excited over the fact I had conned, no, no, talked two of our children into the possibility already and the potential it could hold for our family and future, I had to quash my own excitement. Otherwise, I may present things in a way that would instead of interest my wife, would in fact make her more determined to say no way in hell. Which in all fairness is probably more of the response a normal rational minded adult would have. However, again, I am not one of those. After all, what could go wrong?

Buying property without ever seeing it other than from pictures and images from space, maybe with a few phone calls to people somewhat familiar with the area, while being a 50 year old couple who both have some issues with things and are also not capable to put in hard manual labor without some serious repercussions, sounds like something out of a story book to me. Oh have I yet to mention this property I found is on an island? Only able to be gotten too via a ferry ride, an airplane or in some winters the ice freezes over thick enough you can cross the ice. Perhaps I forgot that part. Well, it is not important. It only sits five miles out into the Straits of Mackinac, at the northwestern edge of Lake Huron where Lake Huron and Lake Michigan meet.

So when she gets herself up and around, I casually mention I found a small chunk of property, that looked pretty cool, that I had sent a link to our son and our daughter both. Perhaps if we all considered going in on it, then perhaps it would be a place for everyone to use as a family for camping. Otherwise, to those of you familiar with fishing, I was chumming the waters and casting directly into the chum line. She loves to camp. She loves to be away up north. She loves to collect rocks and walk beaches. However, for every love, there is also a dislike. She dislikes boats, and she is terrified at the idea of flying.

My wife being married to me over the years is no stranger to half cocked and hairbrained ideas, not to mention we do have four children which means she has had to also deal with their ideas too. So she nodded and asked the next question. "Oh yeah, where at?" I casually gave it the pause that an unexcited individual would before responding, "Bois Blanc Island." She kept doing what she was doing. A few minutes later she returned with,"Where is that?" Ah ha! Interest, I knew it. So, I explained it is the largest island in the straights of Mackinaw, the big one you see when crossing the Mackinac Bridge going north to the land of the yoop. (For those of you not familiar. The Yoop is Michigan's Upper Peninsula and those who live there are more affectionately known as Yoopers.) More silence followed, for a longer period than I had hoped. After all, I am not getting any younger. I have visions going through my head of what I am going to need to live on this island already bouncing like a let loose super ball from my childhood bouncing around inside my skull.

After a while, she again returned to the topic, "How much land and how much money?" She also knows we are not well off. Well to be truthful, we are not well; oh hell, seriously we are nearly one foot in the grave already financially speaking. So, she is fully appreciative of the fact that I am aware of it too. She knows I would not bring this idea up if there was not a plausible chance somehow we could afford such a thing.

So I began the sales pitch. "Well it is a little over one and a half acres of land. The cost total is $2,500." I was cut off with a look out of the corner of her eye and a slight snort. The general meaning is I need to stop. Then a breath, and the "Where would I pull that kind of money out of?" Ah the moment. "Well as I figure it the cost to us would only be around $840." Now I had her hooked. The fight was on. Can I land her, or is this big ol' fish going to straighten the hook, snap the line, or hell it may flip the boat on me and eat me still too.

"Didn't you just say it cost $2,500?" "Yes I did, however, I also have Rion and Mary interested. So, if we all went in and bought this, it would cost each of us about this much. Which they think it would be a great potential for us all to use as a family getaway to go camping and such. Not to mention, when we sell this house in a couple years as we have said we want to do. We would already have property we could build a new smaller house on." I went into over-bearing mode now. I needed to pour it on to overwhelm her and give her lots to ponder. "Think of the smaller home, a place the kids and grandkids can come to, up north where they all can get away and we could live, plus the 34 miles of beach to walk, and the woods to hunt and hike. It even has inland lakes for kayaking and fishing too."

She went back to thinking, and I went back to drinking coffee. "So where did you find this land? What do we know about it and such?" I explained to her that I had been reading up on the island. I told her the island is pretty much un-inhabited. There are only about 50 people who live on the island year round, that you can get to it by ferry, plane, or in winters an ice bridge if its cold enough to freeze over. Her response was, "Well if Rion is interested you must be on to something because he isn't nearly foolish enough to fall into some stupid hairbrained idea you come up with without giving it some rational thought. So, how would we pay for our portion?"

I had done it. I had her interest. Now I needed to bring it all to reality. This would take work; however, it really was a potential possibility. So I told her, "Our tax money. We usually get back around $1,200. We could essentially use that for our portion." She gave a slight nod and returned to her tasks she was paying attention to. "If Mary and Rion are in agreement they are willing to put some money into this too, then I guess we probably could. I had managed it. I landed the fish. Now all I had to do was get the other two that I had on the stringer into the boat, turn the boat towards home and succeed in making it through the building waves of water that this hairbrained idea was turning into. If I could pull it all off, I could have one hell of a feast.

The thought of living on an island, oh, it would be a dream come true.

CHAPTER TWO

From the Heavens.

Now with the permission to proceed into looking into the potential possibility of this hairbrained idea of mine, I need to also explain a few things. I spent a good bit of my life alone. No, not alone as in single, but alone as in with no one around me. I spent a good bit of my working time as an over the road truck driver. I hauled yachts, cabin cruisers and other boats around North America. I would be gone usually four to six weeks at a time, living in a truck all alone, while my wife and kids lived at home. Seclusion has been something I have learned to not only deal with but thrive in. While doing this, I developed a passion for the West. I always wanted to move out west to live in the mountains.

However, a couple of years after my wife and I met, her father passed away. He was a great man for the short time I knew him. Before he passed away, I made him a promise. I promised him that I would make sure my mother-in-law and my sisters-in-law, who still resided at home, would be cared for as best I could. He was ill at the time, and I knew it was a worry of his. When he passed away, my wife and I began taking care of the things we could. None of them drove a car, so we took them to the store, doctors, and did things to help them when they needed help. Leaking roof, or other things like yard work or home care. We did this for nearly 20 years. My mother-in-law passed away nearly two years before I stumbled onto this property. My two sisters-in-law also passed away in this time period.

They, all four, if you include my wife's father, knew I really did not want to live where we did. We always tried our best to never make them feel as if we felt them a burden. As if we only lived here and did what we did because of them. It was not how we felt or who we are. We did it because they were family, and sometimes you sacrifice your own desires to ensure others are cared for. Yet at the same time, if we did not have the deep interest in family first and caring for them and commitment to such, we honestly would likely have moved away. Before we bought our home we lived in, when I found the property. Our biggest discussion when we were looking for a new home was the concern of how far away would be too far for us to continue to care for the three of them.

So with all the aspects of stumbling onto the property for sale, the aspect of getting the kids interested and doing very minimal research and preliminary work that I had performed, looking at multiple satellite imagery sources available to me. Which let me be honest here. Anyone who tells you that one satellite image is the same as another, is also likely to tell you that one breed of dog is the same as any other. Or that there is no such thing as an ugly person because they are all beautiful.

Like it or not, some things just look better than others. Perhaps it is just my old eyesight or perhaps not. All I know is one picture is not the same as another. So one must always consider if there is a better option available. Okay what was I saying again? Oh yeah, I was talking about the process of research. You need to seek out and use all available resources at your disposal.

You may also be realizing I get distracted rather easily. Something my wife loves to remind me of often. So back on topic, later that day I was surprised when handing my wife the mail, I saw a letter from the lawyer's office that was handling the entire affairs of my late mother-in-law's estate.

My wife sat with a look of shock when she opened it. She had received a check, and the estate was finally settled. That sense of sorrow, yet relief settled over both of us. It had been a long and drawn out process that had taxed her emotionally for over a year and a half. Yet here it was, now officially over. Once it all sank in and we began to discuss things, I kind of looked at her and simply said, "I do not know about you, I know I have said for years everything happens for a reason. I just find it kind of odd that for all these years your mom knew we would rather have lived someplace else.

You love the lakes, beaches, looking for rocks, you love the idea of family, grandkids and such. Today, I stumbled blindly into the discovery of a property for sale. Not just a property for sale, but one we could actually pull off the purchase of, if we as a family purchased it with the kids. Then the mail comes today, and this is in the mail. It to me is almost as if Mom, and Dad have just told you. "Go, be happy, you did your job, you fulfilled your promise to us, let us help you." She looked at me and nodded in agreement. Then, she replied that yes, she also found it a little odd. Yet, we would have to do some very serious investigation and research to determine if this would truly be a worthy thing or not to pursue.

She liked the idea, yet it was an awfully big risk and chance, so we needed to be as certain as we could before we actually committed to such a thing. There was a slight fear, and hesitation on her part and I also had to confess on my own as well. As good as this may look, it could honestly turn out to be a horrible thing that could haunt us too. Owning property you can not use and yet still end up being stuck paying taxes on could be crushing to say the least.

I knew that I now had to stop the ever expanding visions of things to come and things that could be, that were going through my head. I needed to get down to actually using logic and plan things out as much as I could and get every bit of information that I could concerning this property and such before I went any further. We were both now committed to looking into it as an actual possibility. However, that possibility could not be something we regretted if there was any way possible to be assured of that. As I mentioned already, our financial situation was not one where we could easily make a mistake with even what many consider merely a small amount of money. To us $850 was a good bit of money.

CHAPTER THREE

Digging up Dirt.

With a wife in agreement, a daughter in agreement along with a son interested, and willing to assist in the purchase, the process of research tipped into full swing. With our son's career, he has access to some things knowledge-wise I am not familiar with, such as soil surveys and other such things. So, we began to pull information from multiple resources available to us.

First on the island itself. What is the island like? Here is where I take a moment to remind everyone, not only are we contemplating buying a property on an island sight unseen, none of us, not my son or my daughter nor my wife and I have ever even been to this island a day in our lives. Once more, seriously what could go wrong I ask? None of us had ever done more than look across the water at this island and even then, we didn't know the name of it. What is the ground soil like? The fauna? Is it higher ground or swamp? What types of trees? I mean a google search told us basic things for sure. However, we were wanting all available information.

The state's own website had information on the island. Well, if you call it that. I kid you not, the State of Michigan the place that thrives on tourism and markets things like Birch Run and its outlet mall to those people from the midwest whom love to spend money, or Frankenmuth for those slightly twisted people who find the idea of a never ending Christmas to be their fantasy of the ultimate life. Or hey how about the cities of Detroit, Grand Haven, Holland, Traverse City and finally everyone's destination location, Mackinac Island. Yes, the State of Michigan does all kinds of touristy write ups and advertising for these places.

However this is the way they describe Bois Blanc Island. "The island is located in the Straits of Mackinac. You can see the Mackinac Bridge from the west side of the island. You can make out the Upper Peninsula from the north shore of the island. It has very few amenities, however it does have a tavern, two chapels, a post office, a one room school, a general store and an airport." Thank you Michigan for this. I honestly can not say enough about this description. It is exactly as you would expect someone who likely has never been somewhere, perhaps not even north of the Bay City area to write about a place.

Or, you can go to other places and learn some of the islands history, general description and make up of the size of the island, and also tells you about how you can get to and from the island. If this doesn't quite tell you much about the island, you can turn around and look at some of the blogs and other tidbits of information out there from people who have visited the island. These you will find entertaining and some may find to be interesting.

Let me give you a gist of the types of things you will stumble upon. The first is from the viewpoint of locals. These are people familiar with the way life is lived in Northern Michigan. Which is a much slower pace than the majority of people are familiar with. They will tell you about the wonderful sunsets, and sunrises, the beautiful old cottages and homes, the old trees, the birds and the flowers. How friendly people are. I should remind you that these are people who already live and appreciate these things. Otherwise known as people like my wife, kids and myself.

The second type of people you will see who have posted things are, how should I put this? Ah let's just say it like it is and like I see it. The Citiot brigade. These are people from cities and towns. They like to shop, they like their lattes, they like convenience, they like being catered too and by damned they think that unless they are being treated as if they are special.

Which I myself think these types of people really are special. They are not one bit happy and they will tell you so. Which they do. Often in many ways. The disdain they have when you do not act as if you are a servant, or are beholden to them. Or the ones who outright like to tell you, "Without people like us spending money you wouldn't be able to live here. It is our money and us spending our money and time here that allow you to even exist." Yes, I have had people make those exact statements to me in the past.

These are the people who blog and remark about how horrible the roads are. I mean can you believe there are gravel roads and a twenty five mile per hour speed limit? "There is only a single tavern and restaurant." the way they word it makes it seem as if they are saying, how dare this be. What about choices? There is a museum but it is small and open only on certain hours. There are lots of offshoots, what might be roads or may be driveways but who dares go down a dirt two track driveway? You can almost hear their thoughts of, "After all we have all seen the horror movies put out by hollywood. You could end up at a location with a family of inbred humans who kill and eat people. There is just nothing there after all."

They usually try to mitigate their disgust, and reproach with comments like, it is quaint and timeless and a place for nature lovers. They also complain that there are only limited means of access to the island. I mean can you believe that there is not, on demand ferry service, that the ferry needs to actually keep a schedule? Or that the other way to get there is via airplane. Which once you do, I mean your at the mercy of whatever, after all there is no place to rent a car even. I even read one person's blog who made the comment it was an expensive mistake and they could check it off their list of places to visit, however they would never return there again. I would like to shake that person's hand and even thank them for the fact they will never return.

So there it is the ability to get quick information, however much of the information is very limited. Now since you are reading this, if you have never been to the island, you should be aware. The island is filled with poisonous rattlesnakes, rabid raccoons, swarms of black flies, and mosquitoes. If you get trapped on the island because you miss the last ferry. Well then you really have trouble. You can sleep at the ferry dock in your vehicle and take your chances on the fact that the population at night all turn into werewolves and roam the island looking for the souls who failed to escape back to the mainland. So that they can inflict their lycanthropy upon them and curse them forevermore.

Or you may if you are lucky enough to find a room in perhaps the only location to rent one. Or even a cottage. Which they will ask you to transfer all of your bank account to an offshore account. This is the means with which the locals continue to fund the school and other things they upkeep to make themselves appear as normal as possible to the terrorists who visit the island. If you still insist you feel the overwhelming need to visit the island after all of that. Well take your chances and please do not say you have not been warned. Remember to drive slowly, wave often and smile. Oh and keep a close eye on the locals because if you catch them just right in the shadows under the trees they may show their true selves and you will catch a glimpse of their werewolf features.

So now with that all said, I had a difficult time finding information, that is unless you know what it is you are seeking. Which in our case was information on things like topography, fauna, water tables, soil solubility, population, things like, power, natural gas, phone lines, building codes and zoning regulations. You know things that a property owner would take interest in knowing. These I was able to find with some more in depth information gathering and phone calls.

So the first thing I did was return to the Department of Natural Resources web site. From there I returned to the page with the information for the parcel of land I was interested in and I read every word on the page and looked at the map they had again. I then pulled up a website that showed me the tax information on all the properties in the entire county. I locate the property on their mapping program. I then returned to several other satellite imagery websites I have saved on my computer. I began to compare them and look closer due to the difference in resolution of them all.

I then found the subdivision records on the State of Michigan's website. I pulled up the official map of the subdivision as it was platted out via survey and recorded in 1920. Which I then cross referenced back through other websites and satellite imagery I could access. I pulled topographical mapping. My son pulled up soil composition charts and water table information. I next contemplated a phone call to a realtor who deals with property in the area.

However, I actually have direct knowledge of a time a realtor acted in a not so kind way to someone. I not knowing them did not want to tip my hat of interest in a property to have it disappear off the market before I could actually get it. The reason was simple. This property looked good, however one and a half acres of land for $2,500. When other parcels of land around it being sold by the same way were priced two, or three, or in some cases even ten times higher. I was very concerned that I was missing something.

I found less than half an acre for $1,500 and it had a vernal pond on almost half of it by what the satellite imagery showed. I felt positive I was either missing something or that this had somehow been priced below value and was a steal just waiting for me to swoop in and snatch up. However, I am not known to be lucky. So my apprehension was huge, and thus I was convinced I must be missing something. This spurred me on to look and search even more.

I ended up making a phone call to a local real estate agent. I discussed the aspect that I had found some property for sale. That this particular subdivision looked pretty wooded and wild. A few homes and a couple two tracks cut for driveways, to get access to cabins and such. This also lead to me confirming that there were some sections that were lower and would likely be wet. However,

I also was told that the one section of the subdivision was higher and almost always dry. Which just so happened to be the information I was seeking. We spoke for a while and I was given valuable information on some of the parts of the island. I was told if he, or their office, could in any way help me to feel free to contact them.

This lead to me then seeking information from the county and the township both. This property was in what was being called a subdivision. However, it showed to be wild and undeveloped at best. So I needed to learn about the possibility of access. I learned that the area was in fact a subdivision in name. That there were no actual roads. That there were some drives and two tracks that people had put in place over the years.

Which then brought me to the questions of the legal access to this property. With the individuals in both the county and the township both accessing the information and seeing where it was that I was looking at purchasing property. Both of the offices confirmed that as a property owner. Provided I had a survey done and I remained in the surveyed road right of way. I could in fact, if I desired cut the roads into the property. The only thing they wanted to be clear about was. I would need to remain in the public roadway's right of way and that just because I cut it into the property would not make the township or the county consider it a public roadway for the sake of upkeep and maintenance. That I would be responsible for the road. This was answer number one.

After reading everything I could on the zoning, building, and restrictions that I could find available. I then made a phone call to the individual in charge of permits for buildings. As the information I had found was stating that even sheds need a permit. I had a pleasant discussion with this individual about the island, the area and location of the property we were considering. We discussed the building permitting process and type of structure I would be interested in. I learned what would and would not be accepted as structures that could be inhabited as far as sleeping in. So that the smallest structure that would be considered a cabin was a 720 square foot area. That it would need to meet code in the aspect of a cabin. Meaning it did not need to have water or power or septic. However no vault toilets otherwise known as outhouses were allowed. So any type of toilet would need to be something acceptable. Which we discussed and found several potential acceptable formats.

I had thought about a shed type structure we would just throw cots and sleeping bags in. He informed me this would not be acceptable and even helped me devise a small cabin that would meet the requirements and not be much more expensive than the shed I had been thinking of. With this I was convinced more now than ever, that this would be a good decision and purchase. Now I needed to convince everyone else that it was.

CHAPTER FOUR

The Final Research.

I now began discussing things a little more seriously with our son. We began looking into any and all the information we could concerning the islands topography as a whole. Through this we decided that at the cost and with the information we had. We now needed to attempt to see what the Department of Natural Resources had for information on the property. I initiated an email to the individual that the web site said to contact for inquiries. At the same time I contacted a title company and ordered a title search. We wanted to be certain that this property would be in the clear with no issues.

The DNR individual replied and informed us that the piece of property was available. He suggested we be sure to do our research. I replied that we were in the process of getting a title search done. Where I was then informed that the property was acquired originally in a tax reclamation. It was then sold to an individual who owned it for over fifty years. Which then the taxes were defaulted on and it once more was acquired by the state of Michigan. That the property had been listed in 2013 for auction. It simply did not sell. So it had been sitting since then as an available property to be purchased outright.

With this completed, I made a phone call to the biologist who oversees the area. This was more informative as we were informed that there is a high population of Massasauga Rattlesnakes. The location of the property is high and dry and the issue with it is that it is thick and completely wild having never been cut as far as he knew. He then pulled up the property on his computer and began to inform me that from what he could see there was no access to this particular piece of property. This was something we originally were concerned with. However, after all the research we had already done, we already knew that this was not the case. That the truth was the map the Department of Natural Resources had of the location of the property was not very accurate.

This we discovered was the most likely reason this property had sat vacant and never been purchased. If you did not do all the research and discover the mapping was incorrect you would be convinced there was no access to the property.

Our next step was to get the title search. We made the trip up to Cheboygan, Michigan and paid for the title search. The title search came back as clear. The DNR were in complete control of the property and should we purchase it, we would be able to purchase title insurance on the property. At this the family began to discuss the issue of if we really wanted to make an offer to purchase the property or not. With some discussion we decided that it would be worthwhile for us to continue forward and make an offer.

I then filled out the paperwork and mailed it into the Department of Natural Resources office in Lansing Michigan that deals with land purchases. We were now in a holding pattern if you will, waiting to see if our offer would be accepted or not. During this time I received a phone call from my friend who works for the Department of Natural Resources. I had reached out to him to help make contact with the biologist I had spoken too. He asked me what the parcel number was we were looking at. I gave it to him and he replied that from what he was seeing the property had been sold.

My heart sank, I had been having thoughts and visions of building a home on the property and moving there. Seeing our future of island life with little interaction from others. It just suffered a nuclear mushroom cloud in my mind. I hung up the phone and decided the only thing I could do was to call the individual in charge of the property sales and inquire. I dialed the phone number and introduced myself. After a couple of moments we both got a laugh as what had happened is, that morning he had accepted our offer. Upon doing that, he went to the web site and flagged the property as sold since he had accepted our offer. Removing it from the properties that were for sale. However, since the deed had not been transferred officially it was still showing up on the web site as it would not be removed from their queue until it was officially sold.

I then informed my buddy what had happened and began to inform the family and friends that we had in fact been in the process of purchasing property and where it was located. Excitement began to turn to reality of the work we were actually facing. As people who did work on our property we bought ten years ago. We were not strangers to uncut and wild lands. I had also helped my grandfather and great grandfather clear and fence land when I was a teenager. So the work of beginning to prepare for what we were about to get into kicked into full swing.

I then decided that I would like one more confirmation of the property. I reached out to the individual who owns a cabin about five hundred feet from our property. I first began with tax records of the property to find the owners name and address. I then began an internet search for the individual. I eventually found several names and decided to take a chance and make a blind call. I made a phone call and got lucky and found the right person on my first call.

I had a discussion with the property owner, where he informed me the property in fact was on higher ground. However, he then asked if I knew anything about the property. I informed him I had never seen it and he got a little quiet. I knew what he was thinking. It is the same thing I would have been thinking.

This individual is buying property simply based on the fact that they found it at a good price. They have never walked it nor seen it. This has got to be some city person who has no clue about what wild land is like. How much work it takes to cut in a road or clear property. This guy has to be completely out of his mind. I laughed and explained to him that our family in fact were aware of the work it would take and what it takes to clear land and prepare it. He then began to laugh with me and stated his concern was exactly what I had thought he was thinking.

So the purchase of our dream property was moving forward. One point six acres of land. Fourteen lots of land that would be divided into four lots each with two held as a location for company to visit in the future and camp. The time to pay for it and begin to ready the chainsaws, weed trimmers, machetes, bug spray and needed items for clearing land and camping while we did it were about to kick into high gear. Here it was March, the ferry would not even begin service until May. Our daughter would not be out of school until June. We had a couple months to prepare and get ready before the real work would begin. Little did I grasp that as one gets older time does not sit still. It instead seems to take on the role of a track and field athlete running a race. That the closer to the finish line you get the faster things begin to move. With my age that meant that I was rounding the final curve and although I may still be plugging along, time and the others around me were increasing their pace and speed to make the final sprint to the end.

CHAPTER FIVE

No turning back.

The paperwork arrived from the State of Michigan about two weeks after we had sent in our offer. So about a week after my phone call which confirmed our offer had been accepted. During this time more pondering and digging was done. The process of second guessing your own decision can be maddening. What were we doing, did we really want to do this, what if? This was one of the more trying times for us. The point you wonder if you are making a good decision. After all buying property sight unseen is not something that most people do. Especially if they are not people who can really afford to make a mistake with even $50 dollars let alone $2,500.

More time observing any and all satellite images trying to determine the species of trees. The basic surrounding aspects of what was or was not on the property in the form of fauna. Research on multiple things. Luckily for myself this also coincided with Maple Season. Which meant I was busy getting trees tapped, and boiler in place and ready to boil along with collecting sap. Added to that, I was involved with my daughters schools robotics team as a mentor.

More learning about the islands roads, trash aspects, policies for ordinances, meeting people from the island and getting in contact with people who reside on and or own property on the island. We also began to attempt to get in contact with the ferry company to get information on their business and services. Learning about fishing, hunting, sights to see, history and pretty much absorbing everything we could concerning the island.

Then came the actual time for the discussion and final decision. We found the property, we had done all we could to determine to the best of our ability to put in a purchase offer. Now it was upon us. Do we complete the purchase of the property and send in the money. Do we really think this is the best decision? The questioning of myself was in overdrive. More discussions and contemplation. We made the final decision to follow through and buy the property. The certified check was done at the bank. We then sent the check and the paperwork back in.

Two weeks later, at the end of March, the paperwork arrived. The Quit Claim Deed was in our possession from the State of Michigan Department of Natural Resources. The paperwork to send to the county was completed and then mailed with payment for the cost of registering the deed in our name. A phone call to the county informed us that the deed would be retained for them for forty five days then returned to us.

So the thoughts of how to actually find the property now became the main focus. I called a surveyor and questioned him about a possible survey in the future. I was also informed that there had been issues with the monuments in the past and that sometimes it took them a day or two in order to confirm and get things right in that section of the island. However, I was also given information that the monuments that were originally placed in the center of the intersection of the platted roads were fairly accurate. I was also told that the surveyor wasn't certain, but he thought they may have placed monuments at each block corner too. Along with original lots. Which were marked in the original survey.

In among the time of all this, I had also been contemplating and planning and thinking of things. I kept telling myself, eventually I would like to build a permanent residence on the island. What would I need to do? After a hundred and one thousand things I came down to the facts. First, I needed to actually get to the island. Then, I would need to actually get to the area, which from there, I would need to actually locate the property.

Should all of that happen I would then need to mark the property. Clear a drive into the property, clean up and clear the property. If that didn't sound like enough work I also realized I needed to try to find a way to fund all this. I pondered the possibility of lottery tickets, casino, or perhaps with luck I could get a phone call from a lawyer about a distant relative who left me an inheritance.

This all failed to be logical or worthy investments and I do not have that much luck. So I returned to polishing petoskey stones and charlevoix stones. Offers to clean out gutters, and do some gardening. Doing all of this only added to my mental check lists of things that I could do. The potential, the possibilities, the future ideas. Which is not usually all that bad for some people. However, when you are in Michigan in Spring it is more like, The Highway To Hell. It is maddening and time seems to never work in your favor. It is either flying past like a jet or dragging like a snail crawls.

The truth though, like everything else in Michigan, Spring may be the Highway To Hell. However, no fear it is Michigan after all. Which means even though it is a highway and it does have multiple lanes. They will have all but one lane closed off causing a twenty five day slow down. Which wouldn't be bad. However, the idiots keep trying to force their way into spring up ahead and they keep getting into issues which cause you to come to a dead stop so the twenty five days it was supposed to take now becomes ninety days. Which will present you with the month of April, and May and half of June gone before you ever get to nice weather which will allow you to do anything other than think about things anyhow.

Which is not a good thing for those of us who deem the best recourse of any thought to be take immediate action and begin getting things done. So there I sat, looking, observing, reading, pondering, planning and if you will stewing over it all. Causing my poor beloved wife to begin to shake her head and roll her eyes and even once exclaim loudly,
"Is that all you are going to do is sit on the computer and stare at pictures of imagery and look for information and such concerning the island?"

I mean seriously, what is it like to live in the head of a fifty year old man with an island infatuation after all? So I began to plan. What would I need to take to the island? What things should I take? Who should go? When should we go? How long should we go? Yes, every one of the questions concerning the planning of an initial trip was what I began to ponder and go over, and over and over. I went over it in my head, I made lists, I made a spreadsheet. I added and removed things. Sometimes several times before the final list was in place.

I then moved on to designing a cabin, one which met the requirements of square footage for zoning and code. Wait, why stop there? I even went on to do a floor plan and such for an actual home. I bounced the ideas for the home off a friend who is an architect. Whom, as we talked and he questioned me on my ideas, even he commented, "Man you have given a lot of thought into this haven't you?"

I had primary heating determined, primary power determined, floor space and air flow for best circulation determined, food storage. Hell, I went so far as to come up with a base design for a greenhouse that would include year round bees for pollination of the vegetables in the green house and allow honey collection. Along with how to have fresh eggs and then keep the ducks or chickens whichever through a long winter inside the greenhouse and how to keep it clean with them in it. Followed with how to store and use the water I would clean it with as a fertilizer base for the plants themselves.

Yes, time in Michigan's spring inside my head was a very, very, dangerous place to be and very trying thing for me. I wanted to do it now and get going. After all, I am not getting any younger.

CHAPTER SIX

The Virgin Trip.

May came and went, the ferry was running to the island. However, with a sixteen year old still in school things were not going to happen with a trip just yet. School ended in June, and I began itching to get out and go see the property. I met a few people online who resided on the island. I also had been in discussion with many people who lived on, or owned property on the island through the internet. I was thus aware of several things.

One the water levels on the island, as was the water levels on the Great Lakes, were up significantly from what it was in the past. They were saying record levels even. Two, the bugs on the island were worse than ever. Mostly due to the wet nature of the spring and a large amount of snow that had fallen over the winter. Which meant prime conditions for the bug populations.

My son and I began to discuss when it was we would head to the island. My poor wife was undecided. She wanted to go, yet she also didn't want to go. Our sixteen year old was of the same mind set. The decision came down when our son simply texted me and said. "I have the next two weeks off. I will be home Sunday. Let's go up on Monday and stay for a couple days and see what we can do." That was fine. However, it was a Friday when he texted me this. Which meant I had exactly two days to prepare. From which I had nothing ready.

So Saturday it began. Gathering clothes, sleeping bags, items I had placed on the list. Chainsaw, Weed Wacker, Blower attachment, machetes, axes, sledge hammer, T-posts, wooden stakes, string, extra chains, bar oil, saw, shovels, camping stuff, bug spray, head nets. Pretty much everything you could think of that we may need or have use of. Sunday arrived and so did our son. We ran to the stores to get some items we still needed. Then attempted to get to sleep.

For me, I had forgotten before bed to go out to the garage and bring up the table we wanted to take. So I tossed and turned, and woke up every hour and reminded myself I still needed to get it. Until at four in the morning I said enough was enough. Got up took the dogs out and grabbed the table. Then proceeded to sip coffee and relax.

About eight in the morning, we began to carry things out and pack up. Finished by nine in the morning due to having it all laid out ahead of time. From here, there was excitement, along with a little bit of nervousness. Not to mention I admit I was having some anxiety issues over the fact that my wife would be staying home. She and I have been together 24/7 for nearly ten years. So it is always strange when we are apart, not to mention being apart for several days.

We pulled out after saying goodbyes, and getting lots of good luck wishes. Heading to the North. Cheboygan, Michigan where we would stop to get the couple items we had forgotten to pick up. Get our passes for the ferry, and then head over to the island on the twelve thirty ferry, arriving on the island around one in the afternoon.

The drive up on a perfect Michigan day. The sun was out the temperature in the high sixties. We had good discussions on the two hour trip. We stopped off in Indian River, got gas, picked up some bottled water and then on to Walmart in Cheboygan. Where we had to get gloves and a couple of odds and ends. Then down to the ferry. We parked, and I got out and figured out where to go in order to purchase our tickets. We however had been under the impression that if you purchased a ticket to put your vehicle on the ferry that you as people in the vehicle were included in that fee. So when they told us the price and we had shocked looks they explained that vehicle charge and per person charge was in place. Which made sense we simply didn't know.

So we purchased our tickets and then we waited for them to begin loading. Where they kindly took our passes and then drove our vehicle up and parked it on the ferry. We walked up onto the ferry and stood around talking and meeting a few other people who were heading over to the island.

There was no question about how high the water was as we stood on the deck of the ferry. There was water behind the breakwall, the water was within a foot of the top of the breakwall. Water was running high. However, we could not have chosen a better day for crossing to the island. Sun out, slight breeze blowing. Then, there it was the engines kicked on. It was official we were about to be underway, destination Bois Blanc Island, Michigan. Where we had never been in our lives, and yet had purchased property. We were already having fun talking with people about our experience concerning the property.

The conversations generally went along the following line. This was to be repeated several times over the next few days for us.

(New people) So how long have you been coming to the island?

(Us) First time.

(New people) Oh it's wonderful you will love it, how long will you be staying?

(Us) two nights

(New people) We have been coming to the island --X-- number or years and purchased a place --X-- number of years ago. We love it.

(Us) Well we are hoping we will too.

(New People) So what brings you out to the island? Visiting, renting a place, just sightseeing?

(Us) We purchased property

(New people) Wait didn't you say this is your first time to the island?

(Us) Yes.

(New People) You purchased property on the island? Didn't you just say you have never been to the island? You have never even seen your property you purchased?

(Us) Yes, that is correct.

This tends to lead to the people looking at one another with looks of uncertainty, as to the mental stability of the two men they were talking too. Which at first made us feel slightly uncomfortable. Until we realized that the reason they had these looks is simply because there are only two types of people and these people have seen both. One you either love the island, or two you hate the island. Those who reside there and own property love it. The solitude, the quiet, the simple life. However, it is filled with bugs, and convenience is not even an option. Let alone a thought. What most consider modern standard amenities. Those on the island know it to be luxury. Yes, there is electricity and cell phone service. However, if you think you are going to run to town for something and come back you have a whole new lesson in things.

This is where with the looks, still being exchanged we both would speak up. Explaining that we actually live in a semi rural area of the state now. That we live a very basic lifestyle that is pretty much like those on the island live. We just do it willingly and not on an island. From here we usually received well wishes and everyone hoped we would like it.

The other one was once we arrived on the island where the conversation would kick off with.

(New people) How long have you been coming to the island?

(Us) Telling them the day and time we arrived or how many hours we have been on the island.

(New people) No not when you got here, how many years have you been coming to the island.

(Us) repeat what we said then state it is our first time on the island

Followed by the above.

So it did lead to some interesting conversations. However, the two of us were excited, and yes, at least one of us, meaning me. Was experiencing a slight bit of anxiety over things.

CHAPTER SEVEN

First Day.

The lines were slipped, and we were underway. The bridge opened, and we began to pass the bridge while talking to a couple who own a cabin on the island. She informed us to be alert of the snakes. As the island hosts the largest number of Massasauga Rattlesnakes, the only venomous snakes in the Great Lakes. We had heard this from several others we had spoken too. Including the Biologist from the Department of Natural Resources whom we inquired about the island, and property with before the purchase.

We occupied our time with idle conversation and picture taking on the thirty minute, five mile ride over the straights between Cheboygan and Bois Blanc Island. I would be amiss if I did not say that the closer we got to the island the more my anxiety began to rise. I expressed as much to our son. Who laughed at me and said he really wasn't too worried because it didn't matter to him provided it was at least good enough to camp on he would be happy.

As we approached the harbor, we both being fisherman began to ponder if there were fish in the harbor and if there was good fishing nearby. As the ferry began to line up for the dock we glanced down to see a King Salmon swim past the ferry about six feet down. Both laughing agreed that the question had now officially been answered.

The ferry docked and we both climbed back into the truck. Which on the rack had two coolers, two seven gallon water jugs, a five gallon can of gas and two shovels. So it was obvious we were up to something.

Upon pulling off the ferry, we stopped to take the touristy picture of the welcome sign on Bois Blanc Island. We then turned to the right heading for the home of one of the people we had met online. We had purchased some potatoes for them, and were bringing them to the island to deliver to them. This is also where we were planning to fill our water jugs. We pulled in and introduced ourselves to them while delivering the potatoes, and began filling jugs of water under the bombardment of the local mosquito population.

The drive there was on a gravel road about a mile from the ferry to their home. Once we left their home we drove along the road heading for the general area of our property. The road skirts the edge of Lake Huron and you pretty much see the lake the whole way. It has some homes or cottages along the way. The speed limit on the island is 25 miles per hour. This helps keep the dust down and is also a nice speed as there is nothing to be in a hurry about anyhow.

We passed the Coast Guard Chapel, an old coast guard boathouse that has been repurposed into a chapel. Then turned down the road that would come to an end closest to our property.

My anxiety had calmed down as everything was nice and pleasant and the roads were dry. We proceeded down the road which was gravel for about one hundred and fifty yards. Then it became a gravel two track. It began to climb ahead up a slight rise and as we peered over the rise we could see that the two track took over. On the right side there was a puddle of water. No big deal. As the road turned back to the left, as we rounded that slight angle the water came over both tracks, leaving the center of the road as the only dry points.

Off the shoulder of the road all you could see was water going out into the woods. We eased into the water on the two track and peered out both side windows. Standing water. The mosquitoes and black flies were swarming the truck. We could see after about one hundred feet the two track rose up again to a higher spot, before going back to water and you could see the end of the road at the neighbors property was grass.

We drove to the end. The grassy area was not flooded but you could tell it was wet. We sat in silence for a few moments before backing up to the rise that was dry. Parking we looked out the windows to the swarming insects. Neither of us said a word. I am certain both of us were thinking the same thing. Myself, about my former wife, he about his soon to be long gone girlfriend. "She is going to murder me." Was about my only thought.

I grabbed my headnet, boots and the insect repellent. Put on the boots headnet and long sleeved shirt. Stepped out and sprayed myself head to toe. Opened the back of the truck and grabbed the machete. Our son by this time had gotten out and was grabbing what he thought he may need. I opened a couple of applications on my phone that I had which would help us get close to the property. Looked up and said, "Well may as well begin cutting a way in,we need to see it anyhow." At that, I walked up to the cedar trees and began hacking a way through the thicker stuff at the edge of the road.

Twenty feet in I came to an area where it thinned out. There was moss in places and very little undergrowth. The best part was the ground was dry. I could see wet areas to the right of me which was the West. However ahead, and to the East it was dry. I only had to cut off a few branches here and there to keep a nice path going. Another hundred feet and I began up a slight rise with thicker growth. I cut a path up and over and before me was water.

I once more had a hesitation, and slight sinking in my gut. I turned to the right leading to the west following the top of the ridge. Somewhere off behind me was my son working his way towards me. Fifty more feet and I stopped. At the end of this slight rise or ridge there was a T-stake. Directly next to the T-stake was an old survey rebar stake with the cap on it. To the East, a line of old orange flags from a survey went away from where I was standing. To the West was a section of about thirty feet of water to the South was water. However, this survey marker was exactly where the one measurement I had calculated showed that there should in fact be a corner.

I yelled back to our son. Whom to be fair, is not quite as agile as I am. I mean seriously I am five foot eight inches and shrinking at fifty years old and weigh a whole 155 pounds. While my son is around six foot, four and closer to 270 pounds. So he takes a slightly larger path and area than I do to move through. Not that I wasn't cutting the trail large enough for him. However, if I came up to trees close together I would knock the branches off and slip between them. Forgetting that what I can slip between he has to attempt to either bend them apart or make a way around them.

So he yelled back, he was trying to get to me, and I should see if I could find anymore. I really think he was just trying to keep me occupied so I didn't get too far ahead of him and lose him. He has a fair sense of direction when he is in the open. However, he has always been easily turned around when under trees and in thick vegetation. Which is likely how he developed the ability to use a sharp whistle to communicate with me when he was a teenager so I could locate where he was while working my way back to wherever he was misplaced.

With all of this we moved onto the search and donate. Search for more information and monuments to help us learn more to locate our property and donate to the local insect population through blood donations. I tell you if the American Red Cross ever figures out a way to work with mosquitoes and then extract the blood they gather they would never need to worry about shortages worldwide again.

CHAPTER EIGHT

Search, seek and wait how the......

A h, the luck of the Irish, er, well okay never mind were not Irish. So anyhow, we felt so lucky with finding the first monument that we began spreading out searching for more. Still only carrying a tape measure, a machete, and some surveyors tape. We began walking. Mind you we had no real idea of what or where we could find another one as we may have found one marker. However, the one we found was in an approximate location of where I through calculations had determined the very center of an intersection of a road would be located. Now I am not a mathematician, however, even I can do simple math. If a roadway is supposed to be 66 feet wide then the center of the intersection to one corner of the intersection should be approximately 46.6 feet at about a 45 degree angle.

So now we were pondering whether the stake we found was a corner or the center of the intersection. We ranged out and walked a bit and failed to find anything so fifteen minutes of walking and stumbling through small cedar trees and fallen dead cedar trees, and avoiding stepping into water we had determined, we were not lucky enough to locate another monument. So we figured we would walk back to the one we found.

Perhaps I should take a moment here to suggest if you are ever unsure of something return to the start and try again. You may get lucky. I realize I am not the first person to suggest this. I just sometimes take longer to come to what is common sense than others sometimes.

So as we walked back towards the stake to reassess the situation, I stepped around a tree, and there in a puddle of water is another survey stake. You would have thought I found gold. I let out a whoop and a cheer. Our son who had already gotten back to the first one turned abruptly. Remember, we were warned to watch out for snakes. Well I am not sure if he thought I found a stake or a snake. As when I yelled I found a stake. He responded with, "Seriously?"

He walked towards me. Again, I am not sure what he was expecting to see. So he glances down and says cool. Now we look at the mapping we have. This doesn't really add up. However, it is in a direct line with the other one according to our mapping program. Which we know has a deviation of its own. Which we also know we are under a fourteen foot variation of our actual location based on the GPS positioning readings we are receiving. So we stop, and contemplate. They are in line with our mapped property lines based on the program yet our property is not known to be surveyed before.

So we take a measurement between them. 70, which is more than the roadways are supposed to be, yet wider than a lot, as each lot is 35 feet by 125 feet. Feeling confident enough we can figure things out we walk back out to the truck to get more gear. Returning with some lath stakes, T-stakes and a few other things including the metal detector and shovel we decide we can likely find the center of the intersection monument.

Upon returning, I dropped the gear I had carried out and walked a bit. I gave it a few minutes and upo hearing off in the distance some metal clanking and some frustrated cussing. I decided to yell out to our son. "Where are you?" He returns with the same, "Where are you?" I laugh and tell him I am standing at the first survey marker we found. I then begin walking towards him figuring he has his hands full and I can help. Only to hear him utter, "Damn it, I can't figure out my bearings in this crap. I must have gotten turned around." So I walk up and grab the T-Stakes, and help him by carrying them back to our agreed upon equipment drop point. Thus leading him back to where he should have been to begin with. Once there we again measured but this time we decided we would consider if this was the intersection we should then go looking for the center monument with the metal detector.

Some quick measurements and some string work and we were where it would be if we were in the right area. Metal detector away. Which consisted of me clearing the ground. Moving branches and dead cedar and other debris. While he swept the area with the detector. And a twenty by twenty box later nothing. We were either in the wrong area or the metal detector sucked. So we decided to walk a bit more looking for the possibility of more markers.

We found a nail with ribbon around it. We found a post,

we found a T-post and we found one more marker. We combed the area, and marked all of the items we found as way points in the GPS. At this point we decided we would walk back down the flag line we found leading to the very first survey stake we found. Upon doing so I found a numbered tag on a small tree. Number 31. We were now beyond confused as nothing was lining up. So we retreated to the truck and I made a phone call to Bois Blanc Island Realty. Where I spoke with Sheila since we had discovered a sign from their office out there on what seemed to be the property across the road from our own property.

She confirmed this property with the sign we had found their sign on, was for sale by their office and its approximate location. I sent her pictures of the survey monuments we found and she said from the looks and description we were in fact in the right area. She wished us luck and said if we needed more help give her a call she would help if she could. So we returned to the area. Picked up the items we had left and decided that we needed to go find a place to make camp.

We had not found our property officially and thus did not feel we should try to pitch camp in the area. We also had never set up the tent we had purchased before. It was a brand new tent. So we decided to call it a day and locate a place to camp for the night. This began with a phone call to our friends who informed us that the North Shore had camping sites. So we headed for the North Shore trail. Twenty minutes of driving we discovered the road was closed. Thus we had to turn around. This meant driving twenty minutes back towards our own property and then all the way back around about twelve more miles at 25 miles an hour.

We drove back past the ferry and decided to stop into Hawks Landing and take a look at the restaurant and store. We then had a chance meeting with Larry the owner whom I had spoken to earlier in the year as he also owns Bois Blanc Island Real Estate. He and I had spoken about the property before we purchased it. He gave us directions to the camp sites and off we went to find them and make camp.

Twenty minutes later we were pulling into a campsite setting up a tent and organizing our home for the next day or two. We got things set up and organized. Sat down and realized we had not eaten all day long. We decided that we were too tired and it was now already nine o'clock at night so we simply made sandwiches and ate potato salad. Called it a night and headed for bed. Listening to the waves along the beach right across the road as we drifted off to sleep.

CHAPTER NINE

Great Plans and the smell of deet.

Waking the next morning was a wonderful feeling. Well other than the pain in the right hip I was suffering from. Seems that my air mattress was more of a slight, and slowly leaking thing that waited until about four a.m. to begin giving out enough for my hip to make contact with the ground. By five a.m. I was firmly upon my hip however my shoulder still had a bit left to go. By six I had decided I may as well get up. Which was a beautiful thing.

I saw the light beginning to show and grabbed my camera. I walked across to the beach, where I was treated to the glorious beginning of a sunrise on the North Shore. To the West was Mackinac Island. To the East was the slowly brightening sky as the sun rose. I began taking pictures. There was a light breeze, the mosquitoes were not too bad. I managed to capture what I felt were some very nice pictures.

I walked back to the tent, and began to prepare to make breakfast. Now what would a camping experience be without eggs, and bacon for breakfast. So I first had to figure out how to set up this camp stove our son brought. Now I know camping and a camp stove seems a little luxurious for some. It did me too. However, with the swarms of the locals outside the screen asking for a blood donation. I was more than willing to try the luxury item over the good ole standby of lighting a fire getting coals, and cooking over them. Something about only having so much blood in my body to begin with

So I managed to assemble the stove and actually figured out how to attach the propane bottle and then light it too. As the pan heated I glanced at the two pounds of bacon we purchased. We really wanted some different bacon, however there was a call on bacon in the Midland Michigan area evidently the morning before we got to the store. Because the bacon was pretty much gone. Well unless you wanted low sodium, or some weird city folk type bacon or that ever so wonderful turkey bacon. So yeah we grabbed the hickory smoked real bacon. The smallest choice being the two pound size.

I accepted, I was cooking two pounds of bacon. I sliced the package open as I would a one pound package, Only to then realize once the deed was done, that there was a ziplock top to the package so you could reclose it. Thus I could have cooked one pound instead, and had some left for the next day. Ah well.

With the Coffee percolating on one burner and the bacon cooking on the other. I settled into the cooking process. While our son began to get himself up and about. Likely aroused by the smell of bacon. He came out and sat down in the chair. I finished the bacon and fried up some eggs for us, and we both sat and ate our breakfast while pondering what it is we would accomplish for the day.

The plan was simple. We felt very good about knowing

where we were pertaining to the corners of the property. After all we found a survey line and multiple markers. We had sat down and assessed the situation, and our findings, we waypointed each marker we found on GPS and could visually see things on the satellite mapping program. We had a very good idea of things now. The plan was to take our gear in, measure the initial survey stakes we found. Double check our math and then see if there were anymore stakes.

As we determined they were seventy feet apart. That would depict two lots. So if they marked every two lots then it should work out. We were slightly confused on the number plate I found the day before. However, it did correspond to the lot numbers based on location on the block of properties to our south. There must have been plates placed on the lots at one time was our best guess. We figured maybe we could also find more.

Once breakfast ended, we arranged our camp, and headed towards civilization. As it was still around eight thirty we figured we would play tourist on the way. I wanted to take pictures of the things on the island to share with my wife, and other children.

We slowly made our way past the old Bible Farm, where I took photos of deer and sandhill cranes together in the field. Then the post office, stopped in to take photos of the fire department and the Sheriff's Deputies office. Then walked into the Township office as it was open. I introduced myself and we spoke for a few minutes. They looked up our name and tax information and handed me our garbage bags for the transfer station and the instructions on how the transfer station worked. We then stopped and took photos of the school, and decided to stop by Hawks Landing for a coffee. It was still early.

After coffee and some conversation, which included more of the questions of, "How long are you staying? How long have you been coming to the island?" Larry the owner however already knew these answers and went about his business with a slight smile as we answered. Upon the shock and mild discussions he came out and asked us straight up. "What do you think about your purchase? Did you find your property?"

I smiled and affirmed we felt very close to being accurate where it was. That we had spoken with Sheila from his office the afternoon before about survey stakes we found. We were in fact heading back to do final figures and such. That we were certain our property was in fact high ground and dry with only possibly a couple corners of wet to it. That in fact we loved it. I told him I wanted to get a survey done, a road in, and begin building. That as far as I was concerned the sooner I moved to the property and island the better.

He smiled and laughed, then added. "I am glad you like it and you are happy. You would likely be surprised how many times we have heard of people buying property on the island sight unseen. They do it every winter. They make that first trip to the island in May or June. They get off the ferry they head towards their property. Some locate it, some do not. However, often enough they are lined up waiting for the next ferry back to the mainland and are listing and selling the property the next day if they even bother to do that."

We laughed as we could seriously appreciate that after seeing what we had when looking around the location of our property. Between the biting insects, the water, the thick wooded landscape. Most people of the more delicate variety, now do not get me wrong here. However, the majority of the population nowadays have no idea of real work. They live in a city where they work a forty hour week and complain how tired and exhausted they are. Some actually work fifty hours. Can you imagine?

They have never undergone clearing of land, putting up a fence or building things on their own. God help you if you mention they may need to be prepared for no form of, as it is deemed convenience. The idea of not just going to the store if you need something or having someone else do something for them is not only beyond imagination it is almost archaic to them. So for most people the thought of what we were doing, or I was planning would be worse to them than planning to go to Mars to live. After all, Mars is at least a new planet, how could anyone choose to do what I was here on Earth?

So after a nice visit and a discussion we headed off to the property to perform our planned activities. However, before we could get out of the truck. We were once again welcomed by the very enthusiastic locals. The black flies and mosquitoes were swarming worse than ever. Which once more meant putting on our boots, long sleeved shirts, and head nets. Grabbing the insect repellent with forty percent deet and proceeding to take a spray shower in hopes to hold them off.

CHAPTER TEN

It worked better in my head.

The plan of the day was go in take a measurement or two then place our T-posts, and wooden stakes. We felt fairly certain where our corners were. So we took the time to write our information on the wooden stakes and grab out spray paint and make things look nice. We planned to set the corners and cut and clean up a spot for camping. This way in the future we could camp on our own property with minimal work of carrying stuff from the roadway to the site.

We began to carry in chainsaws, the other gear and stage it again. Then we took measurements again from the original two survey stakes and we once more decided we should double check things by looking again. So we took a bearing on the line we had strung between these two survey stakes. Walked the seventy feet, and I began to clear some small cedar scrub that had grown up. There it was another survey stake. Well that worked well. So we decided to go another seventy feet and look. A few minutes later we have a fourth survey stake. All of these are seventy feet apart.

So we stop and ponder this again. Seventy feet is two lots. So going with the fact there was a T-post at the first one we presume it must mean it is a corner? If we go with that then we now have identified a series of six lots. As we have the corner then two lots and stake, two lots and stake and lastly two more and a stake.

We begin to think there is likely more stakes, perhaps we should keep looking. So now the original plan is out the window, gone on the slight breeze that wasn't blowing and perhaps had been devoured by the swarm of insects annoyingly buzzing just outside of our headnets.

We again take a bearing and we walk seventy feet. This time the location puts us in the middle of an old cedar stump. We searched the area to no avail. We even dig into the stump. Nothing, now puzzled we think. Okay perhaps yet another seventy feet? Do the work and begin searching again. Behind us by fifteen feet we find old survey tape pieces. However was it from a survey or a hunter? It was laying on the ground and there was not a survey stake anywhere around it.

With this we decided to take a walk back the other way and do some more measurements. We walk back down to the metal tag I found with the number thirty one. We then decided to measure back up to the stake and do the math. We do this. It comes up to equal the footage of the lots. Not a roadway. Now we are more baffled. Because, for the measurements to work according to the plat for the subdivision. The lots footage should, when added also include a road frontage. Yet we are not getting the road frontage in it. So we decided to go back out to the truck and take a break.

As we cool off in the air conditioning and do some figures.

We decide we should walk more and see what else we may find. So we head back out and walk past the tag with the number thirty one. We soon after found a forty. We do some measurements and these add up properly. There is an orange survey tape to our north so we head to it and measure and find a stake in the middle of the lot. In line with the number forty lot. This means they have the corners marked and thus the middle of the block too?

We continue walking and come to the original survey stake of lot eleven on the next road over. So we have successfully located lot forty and eleven. However the lots we located are on the block to the east of our block and on the next street to the north. Yet we have new measurements to work with.

Now we decide to have lunch as it is past one o'clock in the afternoon. We ate our lunch and decided to return to locate those other stakes we found the day before. Then do some more calculations to try to put us closer to where we think our corners are at.

Once we finished lunch, we headed back out and walked to the nail and the posts from the day before. Deciding at this point to see if we could find anymore as there were signs and evidence of the old surveyors in the area. We were looking for and using the old cut off cedar trees to help us identify the lines and find pins and stakes. One of the advantages to cedar taking so long to deteriorate was you could still see the stumps from when they cut the rightaways doing the surveys. I ended up walking two whole blocks over to the next road that had been put in. Which also brought me to an electrical and a phone junction box both.

I made my way back and told our son. He then decided it was time for a ride. We drove out and over to the electrical and phone boxes. When we arrived we then found stakes. T-posts to be more exact and the same kind we had found on the corner. So with some measurements we discovered that the T-posts did in fact mark intersection corners. However, who put them there and if they were correct we didn't know. The only saving grace was next to the one by our corner we found an actual survey marker.

So driving back over we passed a house with someone in the yard. We decided to stop and introduce ourselves and say hello. From this we got some information about the properties and the platted subdivision itself. The individual was the son of the person who cut the road in to the back of the subdivision that we were driving. The cabin at the end of the road was in fact his father's old hunting cabin he had sold. He then informed us of the old original survey markers and told us he had just recently had his own property surveyed. Showing us some of the stakes.

Once more all of this helped us to put some things together. So with confidence now we headed back out. We then with multiple measurements placed our first estimated corner stake. The wooden stake we placed a few feet away had written for all to see. "Estimated corner of block 23 lots 1-14 Thibodeau." This way people who may see it would know it was only an estimate and they need not be concerned too much. We were not saying it was official, it was just an estimate.

From the first we measured off and then were able to do a second measurement to the middle of the block across the road from our corner. We were certain we had found the post marking the halfway point of the block to the east of our own block. Directly across the road. So with that we placed our second post. We then headed down the distance of the fourteen lots on the north side and with much discussion placed the T-post. This is where our son and I had some disagreement with the location. He thought it should be in more I thought it should be out more. We compromised.

As I went back to get the wooden stake the small sledge hammer and a T-Stake. I took the time to grab what I thought were the things we needed. Only to discover I had in fact set the item I went to get down, and came back with what I did not need. This is where my son was able to see I was showing some signs of distress.

I was getting agitated easily and I was making mistakes he knew I usually didn't make. He took the assessment of himself and how he felt and what had just happened and decided it was time to call it a day. We then measured off and placed the last corner post off the one we disagreed over. Then headed for the truck. It was now nearly six in the evening. We had been going in the heat for eight hours in long sleeved shirts, head nets, hats, boots, and through the woods the whole time. Often times in shin deep water.

CHAPTER ELEVEN

Exploring the island.

As we had camp set already and we needed to get fluids in us and cool off. We decided to head towards camp which would take a half hour or more to get too. So we decided to see if we could do a little exploring on the way. The day before when we went North to try to get to the camp sites and take what is called the North Shore Trail. We ran into a dead end as the road was closed near Lake Mary. We stopped and took pictures at Lake Mary as we were there and then had proceeded to turn around and make our way back around where we had stopped and gotten directions to the campsites at Hawks Landing.

So today we decided to cut up Firetower road through the middle of the island. Along this road. Somewhere along this road, the story was that there were three cabins. Supposedly in one of those cabins back in the nineteen thirties, the gangster John Dillinger had spent some time hiding out on the island inside one of them.

We made our way slowly and stopped to take some pictures of ducks and such as we drove along. Enjoying the peace and solitude of the island. We turned up Firetower road and soon left the shoreline and cedar behind. Along with any service for cell phones.

We entered into maple and other hardwoods. The canopy was tall, there were pockets of open areas where the forest had grown into a double canopy leaving the understory somewhat open. Other areas were thicker. Likely from logging in the past which had simply not grown back yet. We passed some roads and drives. Looking to see if we could see the location of these cabins which were supposed to be just off the road a bit.

After a short drive, we saw them on the West side of the road. We pulled over and I grabbed my camera. After all, if the story is true then this is history and I love history. I wanted to capture them on camera before the chance they would deteriorate even more and be lost. I walked up and took several pictures of the nearly deteriorated cabins. Only the remnants of the log walls are still in tact. You can observe in the one either a window or door cornice. We walked along and found all three of the cabins and took photos.

Then walked back up to the truck and climbed in to continue our drive to our campsite. We continued down the road observing and noting the trees that were deadfalls and widowmakers, that should be removed to avoid danger and hazards along the road. We stopped at the shores of Mud Lake and snapped some photos. Then continued on up to the North Shore Drive. We turned onto it and figured we were fairly close to the campsite. We followed along the road at a slow pace. Somewhat because the road was not in the best shape and we didn't want to cause issues with the road.

It had several spots where it was covered in water and had been undercut. Some small trees were down here and there but nothing stopped us from being able to continue down the road. What we thought would take us half an hour turned out to take us nearly two by the time we got done. Finally arriving at our campsite near eight thirty.

We soon began to prepare supper. Beforehand, I pulled out the weed wacker and decided to knock down some of the tall grass around the campsite. A few minutes of this and the grass was trimmed taking away places for the mosquitoes to hide. We then retired to the screened in porch of the tent. I began to cook dinner. We sat down to eat around nine thirty and upon finishing sat relaxing and enjoying the evening as best we could. Seems the mosquitoes had different ideas as they had found a way inside the screened in area of the tents porch.

With the uninvited locals being obnoxious we quickly decided to call it a night. I decided to fill up the second air mattress and stack the two together. Making, as I told my wife, my Princess and the pea bed. Two air mattresses stacked on one another with me on top of them both. Perhaps this would keep me off the ground. We laid there talking for a while when it occurred to me. I was on top of not one but two air mattresses. If they both lost only partial air, I could end up folded inside of them like a hot dog in a bun. I voiced this and we both got a good laugh. Near eleven I decided I would step out to use the facilities one last time. Upon opening the tent, out over the dark waters with the night sky pitch black was a Lake Freighter in full lights.

I reached in grabbed my camera and headed for the beach to take photos. Several photos of the Lake freighter and the lights on Mackinac Island at night. However, the mosquitoes soon drove me back across the road to the safety of the tent again. Where I proceeded to climb atop my bed and go to sleep.

As a reminder, when you are climbing on top of two air mattresses stacked on top of one another and then inside a sleeping bag, this is not a feat just anyone should try. It is best performed by a rodeo clown on video to share with others.

Around three in the morning, we both woke up to a stifling humidity in the tent. Our son decided opening the window on his end should solve this. Which seemed too rather quickly and we both returned to sleep. Until off in the distance a rumble was heard. I woke up to that dazed type of fog when you're not awake yet not asleep. I listened and didn't hear anything else. I figured a brief storm may be passing us to the north and its sound carried over the lake was all.

Suddenly at five am and I know the time as I woke quickly and glanced at my phone. The sky opened up. Thunder banging, bright light from lightning and not rain but a downpour. A new tent untested, not to mention only the rain fly no tarp over us and I confess I was concerned. It was beating off the tent. I opened a weather app on my phone to check the radar. Thinking as it was loading. Well at least I will know if we need to run to the truck or if we may be able to simply wait it out.

The weather radar loaded up and I put my glasses on so I could actually see it. As I hear our son now trying to get the tents window zipped back up. I sit shaking my head. Here is the image of Mackinac Island, Straights of Mackinaw and the Upper Peninsula, Mackinaw City, and Cheboygan area of the lower peninsula. Lots of Lake Huron shown on the radar. There is this dark green and yellow spot.

I zoom in. I now have it showing just Bois Blanc Island on the screen. The only place on the whole Island that has anything on the radar. Is directly over the top of the camp site. It is about a half mile north to south and a mile east to west. It is dark greens and yellows. The center of this bank is passing directly over our heads. Realizing the rest of the island is not going to have any idea it even rained. I could not help but laugh a little at the luck we were experiencing.

As I slept through the night I began to realize that both of the air mattresses were losing air. No problem still not on the ground. Thus, I went to turn over. I got a quick lesson about watching your center of body weight transfer. I nearly fell off them as I moved towards the side, and the air rushed to the higher unweighted sides of both of them. Leaving me on a ramp heading to the floor.

I managed to stop myself and center my weight. Where I returned to sleep. Waking up around sunrise again. This time however I was in the middle of the mattress and as I had foreseen the sides were rising up around me. However, I was still not quite on the ground. Nor sandwiched as I thought possible. Which meant I had succeeded and made it to morning. Mission accomplished.

CHAPTER TWELVE

Departure Day.

After getting up and getting dressed, I stepped out to make coffee. Once I had it started I decided to walk across to the lake. Upon glancing out, the sight was something I had not seen before in summer. It was a June day the sun was rising, to the north there was a cloud bank and the mist was still a vapor cloud in the air hanging over the surface of the lake. It was off in the distance this was taking place. You could make out Mackinac Island clearly, and you could also make out a downbound Lake Freighter clearly. However, the exhaust stack plume was clearly visible in the atmosphere. So it was left trailing the freighter by over a quarter of a mile.

I rushed back, grabbed my camera and saw my son was awake. So I told him he should see this. I returned and took photos of the scene. He followed me down and took some too. We both then returned to the safety of the screened in porch of the tent. Where I began to cook breakfast of burger, onions and eggs into a hash and then make toast. We had decided that today we were done searching for things and we would limit our day to simply making videos and taking pictures of the property and island.

We were scheduled for the five o'clock return ferry to the lower peninsula. So when finished I fired up the leaf blower and dried the tent from the rain early in the morning. We then packed up the camp and tent and packed the truck. Setting aside the things we may need during the day. I walked the beach and looked for a couple rocks and or some beach glass to give to my wife. I also walked down to the camp to the West of ours. There was an old log cabin at the campsite. Roof was gone but the walls were still there. So I took some pictures of it.

I eventually made my way back to the truck and we headed back towards what we call town. Which is Pointe Aux Pins for the island. We enjoyed the drive observing the hardwoods and other varieties of timber. Passing along the shore as we began to head towards the ferry dock. Watching the mergansers in the water. Both of us just enjoyed the entire setting. Relaxed if you will. For today was not a day of stress and work. Our minds were content we had located our property as best we could manage with the time we had. We were both in fact happy that we had made a decision and purchased the property. We had seen it. Now it was time to allow others to see it.

We stopped off again at Hawks Landing and I had some coffee, we grabbed a couple coffee cups as souvenirs. I myself collect them so I enjoy having a coffee cup of places I happen to go to too. I had noticed that the rest of the island was in fact dry. I mentioned to Larry at Hawks Landing about how everything was dry, yet we had been awoken by the thunder storm just over the campsites on the North Shore early in the morning. We all got a good laugh as he replied, "Sort of made you feel like Pig Pen from the Peanuts eh?"

After a short time we climbed into the truck and headed East along the road towards our property. The sun was out, it was a beautiful morning. We got out, put on our head nets, grabbed our cameras and readied our GoPro's. Starting them we headed down the path we had cut and used to go to and from the property.

Once I arrived on the corner, I walked the East line of the property to the south, then turned to the west following the mapping application I had used. I walked the full length of the south side of the property and turned working my way down the west edge to the north side. Then returning to my starting point. I had successfully walked the perimeter of the property.

I then went back down the path I started on and cut in through the property. Working my way back west, turning back east, then back west once more and finally walking what should be the roadway back to the east. I then decided to walk the entire section that should be roadway down to the part that the road is already cut in at. From there I walked the two track roads back to the truck.

Total time took about an hour. Half of which was all just recording our property we had purchased so my wife, family and friends could all see the property. When we were done we put our stuff away and began to head towards Twin Lake, and Thompson Lake. The only two inland lakes we had yet to take pictures of. So we could show them to everyone else. We began to discuss the fact we had finished our planned work and perhaps we could catch the earlier ferry at twelve thirty instead of five o'clock. So I put in a phone call to the ferry and had it confirmed we could catch the earlier one.

With that completed we had roughly two hours. We figured we could easily complete what we desired. We turned up Firetower road once more and drove out to Thompson Lake. Where we saw a very beautiful fishing dock put in place. The water was high and part of the ramp to get to it was under water. Well it was too much to resist. I wanted good pictures of the lake and it would provide that for me. So I kicked off my boots and socks and rolled up my pant legs and waded through the water with my camera in hand.

I began taking pictures of the lake. I then looked down and could see fish. Hmm, I wondered if there were any pike near the dock. So I waded back through the water, put my camera down, opened the tailgate and grabbed my tackle box and fishing pole. Hey we had time and I wanted to try to catch a fish. My son, also being an avid fisherman grabbed his pole and we both began to fish. Trying to catch something.

After about an hour I was growing a tad frustrated. I just wanted a fish. I now didn't care any longer even what kind or how big. Figured even a small bluegill or hell a minnow would suffice. I could at least then say I caught a fish on the island after all. So I set my pole down. Waded back through the water began to look under branches laying in the grass. Sure enough there was my target a good ole live earthworm. I snatched it up and returned to the dock. Grabbed my pole and tied on a small fly and then tipped it with a worm.

Tossed it out to a man made structure you could see out in the water. The line tightened and I simply began to raise the tip. It tugged and I had my first Bois Blanc Island fish. I pulled it up and there it was a small perch. About the size of my hand. I took it off the hook, had my son take a picture of it and then I dropped it back into the water. With time running short now, we decided it was time to pack the poles back away and head towards the ferry.

One thing you have to get used to when on the island is the fact that it takes time to go from one place to another. It may only be a five mile drive, yet that five miles will take you twenty minutes as the whole island has a speed limit of twenty five miles per hour. So you have to learn to adjust your life to this. So we needed thirty minutes to safely make the ferry. We drove back down the road laughing how our plans to visit both lakes turned into not seeing the one lake at all in the trip. Because we discovered a fishing dock.

When we arrived at the ferry dock we had about a ten minute wait and they loaded us onto the ferry. We soon were talking to a couple and their adult son on their way back from the island. Once more we got the questions because of the truck and how it was loaded.

"So were you guys out camping, or working?" We explained we had been on the island for three days and we had purchased property on the island. So we had been at the property. "How long has your family been coming to the island?" We smiled at one another as I stated, "Since Monday around one o'clock." The woman smiled and said, "No not when did you get here, how long or how many years have you and your family been coming to the island?" Now my son laughed and said, "Our first time to the island was Monday when we arrived."

A puzzled look followed. Then the questioning, slightly hesitant voice. "Didn't you say you purchased property on the island?" We both confirmed this as a fact we had in fact purchased property on the island over the winter. "So you had never been to the island, never visited the island, and you purchased property on the island. You bought it without seeing it?" We both were laughing as we had become accustomed to this type of response.

We then had to briefly explain that yes, we had found property for sale on the island. We then decided to consider the purchase and we then spent nearly three or four weeks researching and getting information on the property. That we then purchased the property sight unseen and that this was the first chance we had to go and visit the property.

They were all kind of curious about these two men now. So with some more discussion and some laughs they got to hear how we had in fact spent our time on the island working to locate our property. Once we had done that, we then spent about an hour actually on our property and we were now heading back. That we would now look into an official survey of the property to be absolutely positive about its lines and boundaries. So that we could begin construction on a small cabin in another year and perhaps a permanent residence in two.

By the time we had completed our conversation we were entering the river in Cheboygan. Where we were told to stop by and say hi when we get back to the island and told where they lived. We all said goodbye as the ferry docked. My son and I then made the two and a half hour drive back to my house. Where we unloaded the truck and began to talk to my wife and daughter about our experience. Show them our pictures and I began to work on the video I had made.

The plan was now to take my wife and two daughters up. One of which had also purchased four lots. So they could see the property and the island itself. We also began to make phone calls concerning an official survey. Not to mention plan the next trip for about five or six weeks later. We were told the bugs would not be as bad by then and with luck my wife and other children would love it as much as my son and I had.

CHAPTER THIRTEEN

Turning it over.

The drive home seemed to take a millenium all of its own. Both of us were tired yet still pondering things and ideas for the potential and possibility of what we would like to do concerning the island. We drove the non stop thirty hours, okay it was only two and a half yet it felt like thirty, to my home. Where we went in to see everyone and begin the task of unpacking. Our son had originally thought he would turn around and head the seven hours home that night. However, once we got to the house he decided he wanted to sleep too. So he spent the night.

We talked to my daughter and wife about what we had seen, what we experienced and what our thoughts were. I uploaded the images from my phone and camera along with the video from my GoPro onto the computer. I then began the edit of the video. Excitedly trying to show my wife and daughter the images. I felt as if I was the only child sitting at the circus enjoying the act. My wife glanced over at the pictures as did my daughter. The whole time they would look up glance at it, then turn their attention to their phone or the television. Sometimes they would enter a conversation with our son.

Soon enough it was off to bed. I awoke in the morning still running on the high octane island fuel. Thoughts going non stop of things we could have done, should have done, need to do, might want to try. My son and I were still talking about things we could do or try to do while he was packing his stuff and climbing into the truck to head for home. As he pulled out of the driveway, I admit my heart sank a little. I realized that it was back to reality, and I had no one to share the adventure I had just undergone, that had any idea what I was talking about.

My wife now began to show a little more interest in things as she saw the pictures again and watched the video I had taken. We discussed when it is I would get her, and our two daughters Autumn, and Mary, and our granddaughter up to the island. My plan was a firm five weeks. I would need to save up the money, make a list of all items needed. Then begin to organize everything and have it all prepared and ready to go. Along with ensuring our daughter would have the time off work. As my wife watches our grandchildren for our kids it also meant working with our other daughter to ensure she would have someone to watch our other two grandchildren while we would be gone.

The next couple of weeks were difficult for me. I knew where I wanted to be and my focus was on getting back there. However, I also had several tasks I needed to look into. Our son and I had decided that we would obviously need an actual survey done of the property. Thus, one of my jobs was to find a surveyor that would do the job and not cost us more than it would to launch a rocket with SpaceX. I began with an internet search of surveyors in the Cheboygan area. I selected two of them and initiated contact. I gave the information to both of them and then awaited the response.

First one came in at just about $1,700. The other came back with a little over $2,000. While neither of them were the ideal price range I was hoping for. I did understand the reason for the price. So next I asked for input from friends on the island of which one they would use. I got the response and our decision was made. The decision was the easy part. The difficult part would be the price. Which meant that an official survey would be waiting until next spring. There was just not going to be any way I could afford that much before the season would end on the island.

We agreed we would not build any type of a cabin or shed or anything until a survey was in place. This would prevent us from ever needing to worry about being too close to a property line or worse not on our own property when things were done. The reason for this was not because of anything we had done. It stemmed from the fact our current homes builder had made the mistake when they built the home we live in. This caused an issue with the township and in the end the individual ended up having to give a half acre of land to the neighbor in exchange for a strip of land in a pie wedge of 200 feet long and twenty feet wide at the one end. This way the home would meet the township guidelines for the distance to property lines of the building.

So we knew for a fact that we were not interested in this possible scenario or nightmare. I also was contacted by one of the people I had begun to communicate with from the island. Sheila was the realtor that had helped my son and I via a phone call to her, for help with a question when we were on the island about survey stakes. She inquired if I would be interested in purchasing more property in the area of our current property. I was intrigued and began to ask her about the property she was asking me about. After my first guess, which was wrong, as to the piece, she confirmed my second guess of property to be the correct ones.

I laughed and asked her the price they were seeking. She told me she would look into it and that there was not an actual listing yet just that she had been contacted about a possible future sale of it. I informed her to let me know and keep me informed. That at this time, I would not make an offer, however when we actually did sell our home, I may be interested if the price was right.

We both laughed and she said that was fine so long as I understood there was no way I would get it for the price I paid for our current property. I had begun to realize that we had essentially gotten a steal when we bought our property.

Turned out we paid around $175 per lot. The average rate of money in exchange for lots in that area we had discovered was around $1,000 per lot. Which meant we had already made money so to speak off the investment by simply making the purchase. We were all kind of shocked when we saw how much things were actually selling for compared to what we had paid.

One week rolled by, then a second, soon a third. I realized time was growing short for my plans not to mention the summer itself. After all Mary would be going to college in August. Autumn would be beginning sports in August and school in September. Thus, I put the family on notice. I then prayed for nice weather. Nothing is worse than camping when it is raining and you are living out of a tent with three women and a toddler. The date was set for July 22 to leave home and arrive on the island and leave the island on July 25.

Our daughter Mary put in for her time off and I began

to seriously count pennies for the costs. I then began to plan. What would we need, what was the intent of the trip, what would we take or need for food and such. All of this is something you have to take seriously. You honestly have to be very detailed in your plans when you are heading to the island. There is no way to get things you may have forgotten. So if you need it and did not bring it, the only thing you can do is deal with it or you will have to cross back over to the mainland and then purchase it and return. Which costs a good bit of money.

Mary informed me she had gotten the time off. Our daughter Trina had her babysitting covered and the time was now down to days. I went over the lists, we purchased a few items we still would need. Then it was over the food items with only 24 hours we began cooking. Macaroni salad, potato salad, and coleslaw. Treats of cookies and rice krispie treats. Ice was in the freezers awaiting the packing. The decision of how to pack now was the issue. Did I want to put items on top of the van and strap them down, or try to fit them all inside the van and make for a very uncomfortable ride for three hours both directions. I left this decision to the two who would be sitting in the back.

Jennifer would be in her car seat at two years old so she was covered. The question became did Mary and Autumn want to have seats or would they be content sitting on the floor in the back with the dogs, with everything packed in behind them. Essentially turning our two youngest daughters into sardines.

They opted for the second. Which didn't hurt my feelings too much. Putting things on top of a vehicle is always something I try to avoid. I just do not like having to adjust to the sound difference and always wondering if it is still secure. Not to mention the killing of the fuel mileage that happens when things are on top of a vehicle..

So the packing began. The night before I began to pack. Everything but bedding and coolers were in place. The next day would be nothing more than filling coolers with food and then ice. Packing the bedding in, putting the coolers in. Then shoving two people and three dogs into the van. We also had taken our other two dogs to our other daughters home.

They would be staying there while we were gone. The cats would be fine for a couple days with full food and water dishes. The guinea pig also went to our daughters. With everything in place we pulled out and began our journey.

Everyone seemed excited and fine for the first hour. Then the crowded and uncomfortable aspect began. The dogs were laying down, however, when you have two six month old Great Pyrenese and a Labrador Retriever, along with a 16 year old and a 22 year old in a four foot by five foot area, well things soon become an issue of comfort.

We stopped to allow everyone a break and to stretch. Where my wife decided she would take one of the dogs and put it at her feet. Now they were all uncomfortable for the last hour of the trip.

After arriving in Cheboygan 36 hours later. Well okay it was an hour is all. We did have a 16 year old beginning to suffer from a caffeine headache as she had not had coffee that morning. Which did not stir any feelings of compassion in me as she could have, she simply chose not too. She is however borderline hypoglycemic which means her sugar drops and frankenstein comes out.

So into the store to purchase our bread, and eggs we would need. Along with something to feed to the 16 year old creature we left in the van to help with her sugar issue. Then to the gas station to top off the gas and get her a coffee so she could return to the land of the living. From there it was a simple drive back over the river to the ferry dock.

Our granddaughter and I then went inside to purchase our tickets for the ferry. We returned to the van. Where we were able to convince everyone to get out and spend time on the riverfront stretching and relaxing while we waited for the ferry.

Soon the ferry arrived and they came down and loaded our van on board. We then coaxed the dogs to go up the ramp onto the ferry along with my wife. The dogs were a tad easier to convince to do this than my wife was.

I think I may have mentioned before, if not I will now. My wife really is not fond of boats. She does not swim and well large bodies of water make her nervous. So once the van was loaded and we got onboard. My wife decided the best place for her was in the van. Which I agreed with. I thought she would do much better riding there. The dogs were also loaded in the van and I stood outside of it by the window to talk to my wife through the trip. While our granddaughter and two daughters would wander wherever they desired.

Here we were prepared and loaded and from here it was once more no turning back. Do or die, they would either love the island or they would hate the island. One they would thank me and be happy. The other, well they may bury me on the property or anyplace else on the island. The outcome was in the air and we would all soon know one way or the other which it would be.

CHAPTER
FOURTEEN

First Impressions.

The ferry was loaded, the engines fired and my wife looked over at me with a nervous smile. Our youngest daughter was off halfway to the bow leaning against the bulkhead. Grand daughter sitting in the passenger seat in the van, she had found the cheetos so she was happily munching away. Our older daughter was standing next to me by the van as the bridge rose up and we departed the dock. Out under the bridge down the river. Out across the lake you could see the grey blackish green five miles off of the island. The river was smooth as it would be expected.

As we cleared the mouth of the river the engines increased power and a very audible change in tone happened. My wife glanced at me and I smiled, and simply said more power. There was a slight chop of the waves with one to two foot waves. Mild white capping occuring, I knew if it was like this at shore then the cross channel current would be interesting. My wife glanced over and asked me,

"Why am I getting wet?". I laughed and told her we were taking a light spray from the side of the ferry as the wind and waves hit it as we drove through them. About this time a large wave hit the corner of the bow and water shot upwards in a geyser effect. Spraying the deck and vehicles as she began to roll the window up.

The worst was now upon us in this crossing as the waves could be heard as we hit them every few seconds. The spray was everywhere. I explained, in a few moments we would come behind the island and it would break the wind and the waves would decrease. A few minutes later and all began to subside and the ride became more relaxed for her. Our grand daughter wanted to walk up to the front and look out the gate. So I took her up to see the water. Soon we were pulling into the harbor and back to the vehicle so that we could prepare to disembark from the ferry.

As we all took our places the plan was once more explained to all. We would go to get water, then out to the campsite. They would get to see a little here and there as we drove along, as the campsite was clear across the other side of the island from where we were at. I stopped so they could take photos of the welcome to Bois Blanc Island sign. Then a right turn onto the road. Down to the Schlund's home.

They saw deer along the way which was only a mile from the dock. We arrived and said hello to Clover and Joe. I got out to get water while everyone else stayed in the van. My wife was not in the best mood at the time due to the dogs, the ferry and the kids who had been irritable on the way. Not to mention she is also very shy when it comes to meeting new people.

After getting water and thanking them again for the kindness of allowing us to get water, we began the thirty to forty minute, ten mile drive to the campsite. We drove back past the ferry dock, through the village of Pointe Aux Pins, out past the airport and on out towards Bible Rd. To reach the North shore and the campsite. We drove along at the blinding speed of twenty five miles per hour. Where once we left Pointe Aux Pins the conversation seemed to drift off as everyone was busy watching the woods and try-ing to see what they could see.

When I made the turn out along the North Shore, they could see the lake and then the interest picked up again. Everyone was looking at the beach, the water and the views. I was watching the crashing waves and the winds while passing the campsites thinking oh no. There were people in the campsites and I was surprised as I figured if we got there midweek the odds were we would be able to easily find a campsite. The first one was occupied, the sec-ond one also, the third one was also occupied and my heart began to sink. I really wanted to be in the fourth spot where it's bigger and there is more room. As I approached it I realized no one was in it.

I pulled in and turned the van around. Announced "wel-come home". I climbed out of the van and began to get things going. I had pretty much already told everyone I would put out a rope, put the dogs on the rope so they could move and be out of our way and we wouldn't need to worry about them. Then we would empty out the van. Once it was empty I would set up tents and get things or-ganized and we would then have dinner. Now I remind you it was already seven thirty in the evening when we arrived at the campsite and began this.

I have a wife who has not eaten, two daughters who have not eaten, one of which has some issues with food allergies along with the borderline hypoglycemia, and a two year old. So as we hurry and empty the van and set things out. We get to the tents. I grab the larger one and I begin to set it up. The tent laid out, the poles in place, staked down and up it goes. Everything set the rain fly in place. I turn to grab the tent we would use as a bathroom and the wind laughs, and says Ah no, and flattens the large tent.

At this, I then look, and make a decision to pull one stake and pull the van in front of the tent so as to block the wind from hitting the tent. Then return to putting up the bathroom tent and our daughter and granddaughters tent. The van is working as a wind block and we begin to put things in place. Table , chairs and coolers in the screen porch of the large tent. Bedding, clothes and beds inside the tents. The dry food and snacks inside the tents. I set up the toilet inside the bathroom tent and settled in to boil some hot dogs on the camp stove as there is no possible way to have a fire safely in the winds that are blowing.

Dinner is completed and we set down to relax and stretch as it's been a long and fairly uncomfortable day. Soon enough our granddaughter is off with her mom and their dog to bed. I also discovered when our son and I were up on the island and using the tent, that they really did not put much thought into the screen porch area. The screening has no overhang at the bottom and it doesn't even touch the ground in most areas. Thus I had an idea to put material with safety pins temporarily to test it out. Along the bottom of the screen and extend the bottom and make a sweep if you will that touched the ground and would thus keep bugs from finding their way under the screen and into the porch area.

I cut the material and pinned it into place before dark and then sat back and enjoyed the screened in porch with no insects getting in. The downside was it also made it so there was nearly a knee high spot at the zipper you had to step over to go in and out. Or in the case of the dogs and our granddaughter lift it up and let them go under the screen. Either way it worked to keep the bugs out and that was all that I wanted to have happen to begin with. Our sixteen year old soon enough decided to head to bed and left my wife and I sitting in the screened porch for a half hour or so before we decided to also go to bed.

Once laying on the air mattress the usual aspects of a first night kicked in. Laying there thinking to myself. I need to go to sleep. However, it was a tad difficult when the sounds that could be heard were the crashing of the waves on the shore one hundred feet behind our heads. Along with the winds whipping the tent and rainfly. The sound was like watching a video of the people who climb Mount Everest and they are in their tents at a base camp. Never ending whipping of the material and the winds shearing around it. The gusts would hit and everything would shake even with the van blocking the wind and protecting the tent.

Eventually I managed to doze off and drift into sleep. My wife? Not so much it turns out she had a most difficult time getting to sleep and staying asleep. I would love to say the night passed to morning. However, it did not. Shortly after falling asleep I was startled by explosions. Not the most pleasant way to be awoken as I started up and it came to me I was in a tent and we were on the island. All of this during the continued sound of popping and explosions from my right side. Then it occured to me, fireworks. Some bloody fool was lighting off fireworks.

Now for those of you who enjoy them good for you. I do not enjoy them in the least bit. To be startled awake by them really made me a bit frustrated and angry and I hoped it would not last too long. Which for my sake and honestly most likely there's too as it was not enough to get me out of bed. It ended after a few minutes.

Somewhere in the middle of the night among the winds, our old labrador retriever awoke and began to pace. I reached over turned on the light and she was all over the tent in a somewhat confused and agitated state. I got up, found my shoes and took her out. She did her thing and then did not want to return to the tent. She sat down and looked at me as if to say. I am old, I am too old for this crap, why did I have to come with. I don't even know where I am and this is not fun.

After a little coaxing she agreed to return to the tent. Some of which was me nudging her in the rear end with my foot to make her go back inside the porch area leading to the tent door. While she gave me dirty looks. Once inside, the great pyrenees pup wanted out. I say pup, however she is six months old and already bigger than our labs. So I then took her out too and returned.

I was eventually able to return to sleep. This would be a glorious sleep. Well if sleep would have been unhindered. However, as if to say welcome back to the island, just as it did the one night our son and I were there. Mother Nature decided that it would only be appropriate to greet us.

I was stirred from slumber once more this time in that foggy sort of way. The winds had died down. Oh thank goodness was my thought. Then that thought no sooner echoed through my skull when I paused. What had I heard? Was that thunder off in the distance? No it can not be. I strained to listen, yes there it was again. I reached for my phone to check the weather and radar.

Sure enough a band of rain was blowing in over the straits of Mackinac. We soon would experience about an hour's worth of rain. It was around five in the morning when this was kicking off and I decided I would not bother getting out of bed to begin my day until it ended. I managed to doze off again.

CHAPTER FIFTEEN

Make it Memorable.

As I pulled myself out of the sleeping bag and managed to get dressed, get coffee going, I then remembered it was also a very important day. It was my wife's birthday. So I wished her a happy birthday. Her first birthday on the island and turning fifty at that. What a great thing in my view. Well once more that was my view. Turns out she wasn't so happy to turn fifty after all.

I then began to make the bacon, some toast and scrambled eggs. We fed the dogs and cleaned up our camp. With breakfast out of the way and the coolers loaded so we would have lunch meats and other stuff with us for eating during the day. It was time to decide how we would go about touring the island. We decided that we would just more or less do whatever came to mind with the biggest thing being we would go to the property sometime during the day so that they could all see it.

As we loaded into the van and I started it, I simply asked Left or Right. The initial response being, "What?" I repeated myself. Where I then received the response of, "Well I don't know what is where?" I said well to the left if we head back down we can go to the West end of the island or on back through the village and along the south shore. To the right we follow the North Shore Rd. Until we get to Firetower Rd. Then we head on down through the middle of the island and decide when we get down there. I then said the only thing we had to do was stop and fill up the other water jug sometime during the day.

At this, my wife announced to the right. Which as it was her special day, I pulled out and turned right. We made our way slowly along the road. Windows down enjoying the breeze off the lake. When the deer flies made their arrival. As they began to swarm the van, I rolled the windows up and turned on the air conditioner. Making our way along when in front of us soon enough was a water hole. From taking this road with our son in the pickup I knew they were gravel bottomed and thus I simply drove along not worrying.

We made our way all the way down to a set of homes or cabins where the road makes a turn to the south, after the turn ahead of us was a set of gates. My wife asked if we could pass them? I informed her, no the road turns to the left just before them. We made the turn and the road became a two track and climbed uphill. Here is where most people would likely get nervous. However my wife is married to me and has been for a lot of years. More than she would like to admit most of the time.

So she is used to me taking vehicles not made for these kinds of adventures down roads and trails. So as the branches and trees closed in on the trail and I continued to just drive along at a nice slow pace we climbed the elevated gravel two tracks over rocks roots and stumps. Branches scraping along the sides of the vehicle. Giving the shocks and struts a nice workout.

We eventually came over a slight rise to find a small all terrain vehicle and a quad approaching us. There was simply a two track, trees everywhere and not anyplace a mini van is going to move off the side of the trail. I stopped and the two individuals stopped. Both kind of looking at the van as if the thought was,"Who the hell would take that down these trails." They both moved off the side and I smiled and waved and said thank you as we passed them. I glanced in the mirror as they returned to the trail looking back at us. I am certain they were still thinking, "This stupid tourist is lost and has no idea what it is they are doing." So we continued on our way to Firetower road.

A bit later turning South on firetower we began to make our way up over the backbone of the island. The granddaughter had dozed off which was a blessing as she was very cranky and getting on everyone's nerves. Honestly, this is an understatement. It was more like I was thinking we had trapped a werewolf in a child's car seat and it was fighting to get free, howling and snapping the whole time. Until it was tranquilized and became quiet. Either way we all kept our hands clear of her mouth as she has been known to bite.

I turned down the trail to mud lake. Stopping to let everyone see the lake if they chose. Then backed out and down the road back to firetower road. Turning to the right and slowing as I approached the three deteriorating cabins that are referred to as the Dillinger cabins. Where our sixteen year old who has a love and adoration for history as much as I do jumped out to go investigate. When she was done we continued on down the road and I turned off to take them to Thompson lake.

We got out of the van and went to the dock, everyone was excited to see the lake and dock and enjoy the views. We saw a couple kayakers who were coming out of the lake and we had a brief conversation with them concerning the dogs. After climbing back into the van to continue our drive. We eventually reached Huron Drive where I turned to the left in order to head towards our property. Everyone was now enjoying the lake shore and views as we made our way along.

I decided to stop at Snow Beach to let our granddaughter and dogs stretch their legs. The water was calm, the sun was out. They enjoyed this brief stop and then it was back in and down to our property. Which to get there meant a short drive yet. We approached the Coast Guard Chapel as I slowed down. I stated that if the road went on through this would be the road that leads down to our property. However, it did not. So we went to the next road which leads back by our property.

I began easing down the road, telling everyone with me about who lived where and who it was our son and I met when we were up. I slowed to tell them where the water was at compared to road a little over a month ago. I was also looking to see how bad it was compared to when I was up last. I was very happy the roads were dry, the woods looked dry. When we got to the part of the road that was nearly flooded over when I was there last, I was actually surprised to see it dry. When we got to where my son and I parked in the only dry spot in the area, when he and I were there. I began to laugh and explain to them how bad it was. From there I drove to the end. Where I received a pleasant surprise, our neighbor was up on the island and at his cabin.

I parked and got out of the vehicle. Where I then introduced myself to him and he began to laugh. He said he wondered about me and if I had actually gone through with the purchase. This was the individual whom I had made a blind phone call too back in the early spring. I had found his phone number on the internet and actually succeeded in making the correct call on the first try. We had discussed the area around his property to try to determine the likelihood it was a dry piece and not a swamp. We had a very nice talk. Turned out that he and I had a lot in common other than the property on the island so that helped.

Everyone got out of the van, and we sprayed down with mosquito repellant. In the meantime our granddaughter took a liking to him and was following him around. We all visited a bit. He told us to feel free to park on his property and go enjoy ourselves. At that we took a walk down the trails our son and I had cut into the woods and marked with the survey tape. The dogs were a bit of a hassle. As we walked into the property I kept laughing as I told them what Rion and I had gone through and experienced when we were there. Our impressions at the time and what we had seen. After a short walk we arrived at the first stake that Rion and I had found. I then lead them over to where Rion and I estimated our first corner to be located.

I had brought a can of bright orange paint with me in case I wanted to paint lines or posts. I was happy I had chosen to do so as the stakes with the purple paint were actually a tad difficult to see. So I painted the bottom two thirds of the stakes with bright orange paint to help us better locate them in the future. I then lead everyone down to the second stake along the property line, and then down the length of the property to the third one. I was trying to take my time as much as possible as we had three dogs, one of which was older and a two year old child. However, I did have to stop several times. Which was okay with me.

Once we arrived at the fourth corner and I then gave them

a moment to glance around and see around us. I explained that the other areas around us are what I had been informed may be for sale in the future. That we could possibly pick that property if it came up for the right price. We then walked back a little bit further and then down what would be the roadway between our property and our neighbors we had just met. When we finished our little walk, which ended more so because our mosquito repellant was beginning to wear off and they were showing up around us, and beginning to bite more than anything else. We returned to the first corner stake and then walked back out.

As we arrived back at Tom's he inquired to what everyone thought about the property and island. We spent nearly an hour talking with him and visiting. It was now beginning to get into the afternoon and I wanted to be sure we got back to the camp in time to enjoy camping and the lake shore too. So we said our goodbyes and climbed back into the van. We drove back down to Huron drive and turned towards the ferry dock. I listened to everyone talk about the property and how we were all wanting to have a fire, after a day of driving around. It was now just going to be everyone sitting around and getting some time to relax.

We stopped back at Clover and Joe's and got some water. Then I figured we could stop off at Hawks Landing and let everyone see the gift shop and store. However, when we arrived there, the sign said it was closed for the day. This made me laugh a bit. We climbed back in and continued our drive. During the day I had stopped and picked up a chunk of dead wood I could cut up for firewood that night and I had put it on top of our minivan. So all day long we had driven around with this log on top. Now on our way back towards the camp site. I began to look for a few more pieces of wood. Which were easily found.

Back at the campsite. We were prepared to have chicken over the fire. However, the chicken decided it did not want to cooperate. It was still frozen. So we ended up with lunchmeat sandwiches, and potato and macaroni salad. I then cut some wood, while my wife started a fire and we roasted some marshmallows. The day had been beautiful. The sun had been shining and there had not been much wind. Well that is for the South and East side of the island. We discovered that on the island if you do not like the weather much as far as wind goes. Simply go to the other side for the day.

What we were experiencing were strong winds and strong waves again. Not quite as bad as the night before, however strong enough again that I parked the van in front of the tent to break the wind.

We settled down and everyone headed to bed early, after all none of us slept well the night before and it had been kind of a long day. So we once again drifted off to sleep to the sound of waves crashing on the shoreline and beach. My thought was this should be a really good setup for some nice stones and beach glass if this ever stops and calms down.

CHAPTER SIXTEEN

It's all New to us.

O nce more I was awoken in the early morning again
by the dog. Which I begrudgingly took out where I
discovered the sky was clear and the stars were
out in force. This helped me get over my frustration with
the dog. Truth be told I forgot about the dog until it tugged
me to go back in.Which meant it had become satisfied that
no strange things had invaded our campsite. The one thing
I had noticed was the wind had stopped, the lake was si-
lent. I quickly drifted off to sleep again.

When I woke up it was still early. I got dressed and took
myself and the dogs out then started my coffee. I put the
dogs back in the tent and took a walk along the beach a
short distance. After I returned, I fired up the stove and
began breakfast again. Bacon on, and soon enough everyone was up and in the screened porch. I cooked eggs again
for those who wanted them. Cereal for the others. Once
breakfast was over we cleaned up camp and prepared for
another day on the island of looking around to see what we
could discover.

The day began with a trip to the west end. Our campsite

was towards the West end but on the North side of the island the waves were small. We left camp only to realize a mile down the road I had forgotten the camera at camp. So I returned to get it. The reason was simple, I had seen the pitcher plants and I wanted to take photos of them. So with a camera in hand, I returned to them and got out and took pictures.

From there we made our way down to Lime Kiln Point Rd. We turned to the West end of the island. I had never seen the West end nor had anyone else in the van. So we enjoyed the trip through the trees and the new sights. Which in case you are wondering is mostly trees. Upon arrival at the end of the road. I parked and got out with a camera and took some photos. The wind was out of the southwest and the waves were pummeling the shoreline.

I then decided to continue on to North Lakeshore Drive which ended quickly, and at the end of it we turned around. To begin our trip back towards Pointe Aux Pins. Along the way we stopped to take some photos of the tree covered roadway, the airport and the old cement truck. We drove along enjoying it all and simply taking in the fresh air and the beauty of the island.

I stopped by the Museum and dropped off two ships spikes I had found the summer before when snorkeling. I had thought I could keep them, however truth be told I liked the idea of sharing them with others and I would always know where to find them.

With that done, we stopped in at Hawks Landing again. This time for a coffee and a lemonade. Then on towards the property. We had gotten a late start anyhow. We took our time and soon enough there were some clouds forming and the day suddenly became overcast.

I turned down Florence when we got to the Coast Guard

Chapel, however not towards our property but towards the lake. I wanted to get a glimpse of what it was like at the access point we supposedly shared with others of the area. At the end of the road there was a spot big enough to park the van. There was a slight drive to the right. However, it led to houses and I didn't want to impose on anyone so I parked where the road stopped.

I got out to walk towards the shore of Lake Huron, and found my way blocked by a pool of water. I glanced at the mapping program I could see that to my left was the access property to the right was private. There was a quad trail that led through the puddle and I knew it would be a solid bottom. However, I wanted to find a way to walk to the shore of Lake Huron without getting wet.

So my granddaughter, older daughter and I, all began the walk around it to the left. We soon found our way to the lakeshore. Upon walking out from the trees we were greeted by rain. Through the light rain we walked along the rocky beach area down to where we had parked. We now stood on the opposite side of the watery area from the van.

Content I had located and found it we began to see if there was an easier way to get to the van that would not take us directly onto someone else's property. It turns out there was not a way to do so. I began walking back and it was still a light rain So I decided to simply walk through the water. So I took off my shoes and socks, pulled up my pant legs on my jeans. Handed my shoes to my daughter and lifted my granddaughter to my shoulders. I stepped into the water and went on accross. It was only shin deep. Upon getting to the other side I continued to the van barefoot.

Once back in the van we drove back out to Huron, then crossed it staying on Florence. I drove as far down it as possible which was about to the end of the first what should be a block. I then drove back down it and out and around to Dorthy. Explaining the whole time that our son and I had been contemplating the best path to take to set the drive into the property. We were thinking it would be best if we went down Dorthy to Wyandotte then back over to Florence and cut up Florence to our property. The reason being that there was already a partial road up Florence at that location.

How it should allow us easier access and the ability to run power and phone up the road to our property much easier. However, the other options would be to run up Dorthy all the way to where Sandwich was supposed to intersect then cut sandwich in from Dorthy. With the least desirable to simply cut all the way up Florence to the property. It would eventually come down to cost and what would be the cheapest and most feasible when we decided to actually do this.

Our original plan had been on going back to visit with our neighbor, however with the rain falling we decided we didn't want to impose as we would only be able to visit if we were in his home or standing out in the rain. So we headed towards Lake Mary. Once there I pulled up to the end of the road and we simply looked at it then decided we would take what my program said was Drew rd, Lincoln Park Blvd to Redwing drive and back out to Firetower rd.

We turned down Drew Rd, Lincoln Park Blvd and headed into the woods. This trail quickly became two track. Which as before does not intimidate us nor our offroad Mini van in the least bit. We drove along on the very narrow trail with the branches bouncing off the sides of the van. Up and around, around and up and down as the trail twisted along through the woods. It was a very beautiful drive. We came out into a marsh that the trail cut directly across at one point and it was very pretty. Eventually, we did make it back to Firetower road. However, I will tell you now. Had it been wet it would have been a much different experience.

Once we connected up on the main road again a poll was taken. I refused to accept the votes of the dogs or the two year old if they did not agree with me. The Captain of this expedition. So I put it before them all, do we head back someplace else or head for camp and enjoy the lake and the campsite and have a fire. This would be our last night on the island this trip. It was quickly decided especially by our granddaughter when she was told she could get in the water.

So we decided it was back to camp. With that said we headed back out towards Pointe Aux Pins the quickest way to get to camp. Once past the village we began to look for wood for firewood again. We drove along stopping when we found suitable wood along the edge of the roadway and put it on top of the van. By the time we reached Bible rd the van top was full of wood. The length of the roof top and some a bit longer.

We arrived back at camp and unloaded the wood, put the dogs on the lead we had set up. Then as I began to prepare for making dinner the rest went to the lake. The fire was going as I cut wood and piled it. Once I tried and got help from the fire boss and daughter both. I did take a couple breaks and when just about done after sweating a lot. I decided it was time for a dip in the lake and to clean up. About this time a vehicle pulled up and stopped. Asked how long we would be camping as there was a large group of them together and they were hoping to try to camp close together. Part of the group had already taken the site next to ours.

I informed them we were leaving the next morning. However, instead of having to wait for us to leave. If they would like they could put a tent up on the site. Which they would then have their tent on site when we left ensuring they would have the location. They were greatly appreciative of this and we were happy to oblige them. They returned shortly to put the tent up and went to spend the night with their friends.

While my wife Toni, our older daughter, and granddaughter were down playing in the lake. My wife found some beach glass, one of which was red. As searching for beach glass is a pastime of ours as a family. We turn it into a small competition of who can find the most pieces when we are on a beach. Our youngest daughter decided to go take a walk down the beach to look for rocks and glass. She returned with some too. About this time supper of burgers and chicken were completed over the fire. So we all took time to eat.

It was now time for my walk down the beach, and our youngest and I walked about a quarter mile down the road, cut to the beach and began to work our way along the beach looking for rocks and glass. I found a tether ball that had washed up onto the beach lost from who knows where. So I picked it up and we laughed as I named it Roy. We were on an island and I found a ball. Which reminded us of the Tom Hanks movie, Cast Away. Where he found the volleyball washed up on the beach and called it Wilson. So with Roy in hand we made our way along.

I jokingly teased her about how I walked a beach and the only thing I had found was a stupid ball. When I found my first piece of glass. Then it was a long stretch before I found more. However, the area I found my next piece in provided about six more pieces, one of which was a nice blue. Upon arriving back at camp I presented my wife with the glass and our granddaughter grabbed Roy. With the evening setting in we decided it was time for some fruit pies over the fire and marshmallows. Which then lead into bed time for our granddaughter.

I had told my wife about the stars I saw during the night when the dog woke me up. So we figured perhaps we would stay up to see if they came out again. While waiting as the sun set and darkness began to grow, I had the idea of perhaps we should go take the lantern to the lake and see if we could see any glass as the waves had begun to subside.

Taking lantern in hand to the lakeshore with no wind now turned out to be a very poor idea. The flying insects were drawn to the light which quickly became an impossible situation. There were so many that they were everywhere in our faces, all over our arms and hands. I turned off the lights and gave up that idea. We decided to return to camp and to call it a night.

After taking the dogs out and curling under the sleeping bag, I quickly fell to sleep. At which point for the first time I was not awoken by a dog in the middle of the night, no fireworks, no rain, no whipping winds. Just a nice relaxing night of slumber.

CHAPTER
SEVENTEEN

The final hours.

As daylight arrived, I awoke and was unable to return to sleep. I knew I had a lot to do and a short time to do it. I had to get breakfast for everyone, and then move everything out of the tents. Then I would need to take the tents down and begin to pack it all back inside the van. All of which would need to be completed no later than eleven thirty in the morning as we were scheduled to be on the twelve thirty ferry to return to the mainland. With that I rolled over, found clothes and got dressed. Found my shoes and took the dogs outside.

From there it was on to starting the coffee and bacon. A couple people wanted eggs so I made some eggs to go along with the bacon again. Once breakfast was over we began to take everything out of the screen porch section of the large tent. Then out of the tent itself. Everything was quickly happening and going smoothly. We had the large tent down and our daughter and granddaughters small tent down. I took down the bathroom tent and all was good.

Packed nicely as the van began to be packed.

Things were going great, until the toilet we had been using. To save all of us the horror I underwent let us just say that the five gallon bucket with the toilet bags that you can purchase work very well. You can put a dryer sheet in the bottom of the bucket which helps eliminate any odor in the bucket. The bags work well also. They are self contained and you can add cat litter to the toilet as you use it to keep everything nice. However, I stress this. No matter who you are if you use them remember that depending on the number in the party using them. You should change the bag at least daily. Perhaps more than one a day in some cases.

As I said everything was going well. Until I had to deal with that. Where things did not go well. In the end a hole ended up in the bags that they should be in. Which ended up in the garbage bag that we would be disposing of. However, let us just say that no matter how much you wash with soap and or hand sanitizer. Some smells simply do not go away easily. So with the garbage bag full, the van packed we found we still had time. I planned on stopping at the transfer station to deposit our garbage as I had placed the garbage in our township bags we received as property owners on the island.

We went looking for beach glass and stones again for an hour or so. We did find some and when done we returned to the van and pulled out to head for town, garbage bag on top of the van. We arrived at the transfer station and the sign said "Closed." I looked and discovered I was exactly seven minutes late. So now this bag of refuse which was quite ripe would need to travel back over on the ferry with us. We did manage to find a second garbage bag which I was able to get the other to fit inside of. I then tied the bag down on top of the van. This did help eliminate some of the odor.

My daughter decided she wanted to go to the gift shop at Hawks Landing before we left the island so I returned to Hawks Landing. She went inside and purchased our grand-daughter a shirt. Then it was back to the dock to await the ferry. Once we were loaded onto the ferry we sat back and relaxed in the van as we watched the island getting smaller and smaller as the distance grew between us and the is-land. We were content in a way.

Yes, we all loved the island which was a good thing. However, camping in a tent with three dogs and for three nights was a good time limit, based upon the things we had done while there. The mission was to see the island and show everyone the property along with as much of the is-land as possible and hope they all liked it as much as our son and I had.

On that level the trip was a success. Everyone did in fact enjoy it and desired to spend more time there. The plan now was to try to make one or two more trips up before the end of the season which would end in November. For us it would be ending in mid to late October due to the tem-peratures. We all agreed the next step as far as the property would go, would be to have an official survey done. So we would know the actual property boundaries.

We also would then go and clear off a location for a small cabin to be built as a group funded project and location for all of us to stay at when on the island. Which would make our stay on the island much more pleasant as we would not need to then pack so much. We would then be able to stock the cabin with dishes and such and only need to plan to bring clothing and food when we went. I had a cabin design completed already that would work and would meet the minimum required size for permits and zoning.

My wife had also agreed it would be a very nice place to build a home and live for the next chapter of our lives. So a cabin would indeed give us a location to stay at while we actually had a home built for us. As our plan would be to sell our current home and then have a home built for us. We would either stay in the cabin or come up with some-place else to reside while it was being built. Most likely we would stay in the cabin and assist in the construction of the house as we both have the ability to do some work. We had after all refinished the home we own and live in now. Which was in need of remodeling work inside before we could move in.

Our son being an electrical engineer could assist with the wiring and he and I both know how to do PVC plumbing and carpentry work. So we arrived at home only to begin to prepare, plan and think on what and how to go about implementing the next stage of our lives as a family. The only thing we know is that within the next couple of years you will know where to find us and how to contact us.

You can take a ferry, you can risk the ice, you can fly on a plane, or even call, text message and or email. For all of the rest if you still are not sure how to go about contacting me. The only thing I can say is send it by pigeon somehow some way and someday we may get it. For certain though in due time we will be residing on an island in the middle of the straits of Mackinac. Where just a year ago, we didn't know there was an Island known as Bois Blanc Island, or even in its existence. Yet here it is a year later and we have made friends, visited twice and even purchased property and are planning on a cabin and home to reside year round.

Who knows, maybe the next thing I write about will be the grand adventure of a cabin and a house and then moving to an island. If not I hope you at least enjoyed this and found it entertaining.

Appendix

I am including this section for the sake of making the resources that we used in researching information on our property more easy for others to see. I hope it will possibly help others who seek to purchase property as we did.

Satellite Imagery.

Google Earth   www.google.com/earth
Fetch   https://app.fetchgis.com
Bing Maps   www.bing.com/maps
OnXmaps   www.onxmps.com

Resource information

State of Michigan   www.Michigan.gov
Wikipedia   https://.en.wikipedia.org
Bois Blanc Township www.boisblanctownship.org
Mackinac County   www.mackinaccounty.net
Bois Blanc Island Site https://Bois-blanc.com
Various blogs and news clippings found on the web. Too many to list individually.

Phone Calls

Mackinac County
Bois Blanc Township offices.
Department of Natural Resources Land sales office
Department of Natural Resources Gaylord Unit Office.
Where I spoke to biologists, and foresters that oversee the area.
Neighbors around the property.
Local Real Estate Office
Title Insurance and Search Company
Transportation Company
Zoning Inspector's and Enforcement personnel for both county and township.

If you put in the time and effort you will be able to get a fair idea of a property. Again buying property sight unseen is not for everyone, and can be a huge risk. However we are proof that it can be done successfully. We wish you luck in your own adventures if you choose to do as we have.

ABOUT THE AUTHOR

Bruce William Thibodeau

Bruce Thibodeau has lived most of life in Michigan. Having worked in many industries in his life, which most of his working years were spent in transportation. Growing up in Port Huron Michigan area, and spending the last 30 years in the Mid Michigan region. Father of six human children and a number of four legged ones. He prefers to spend his time in the outdoors. Mountain Biking, Kayaking, Hunting, Fishing, Hiking, and pursuing hobbies such as rock and beach glass hunting or wood working.

www.ingramcontent.com/pod-product-compliance
Lightning Source LLC
Chambersburg PA
CBHW032004060426
42449CB00031B/309

9 780578 659459